# BOOK 5

# LEARNING AND LANGUAGE

The Open University

This publication forms part of an Open University course SD226 *Biological Psychology: Exploring the Brain*. The complete list of texts which make up this course can be found on the back cover. Details of this and other Open University courses can be obtained from the Course Information and Advice Centre, PO Box 724, The Open University, Milton Keynes MK7 6ZS, United Kingdom: tel. +44 (0)1908 653231, e-mail general-enquiries@open.ac.uk

Alternatively, you may visit the Open University website at http://www.open.ac.uk where you can learn more about the wide range of courses and packs offered at all levels by The Open University.

To purchase a selection of Open University course materials visit the webshop at www.ouw.co.uk, or contact Open University Worldwide, Michael Young Building, Walton Hall, Milton Keynes MK7 6AA, United Kingdom for a brochure: tel. +44 (0)1908 858785; fax +44 (0)1908 858787; e-mail ouwenq@open.ac.uk

The Open University
Walton Hall, Milton Keynes
MK7 6AA

First published 2004

Edited, designed and typeset by The Open University.

Printed and bound in the United Kingdom by the Alden Group, Oxford.

ISBN 0 7492 6627 9

1.1

# SD226 COURSE TEAM

## Course Team Chair

Miranda Dyson

## Academic Editor

Heather McLannahan

## Course Managers

Alastair Ewing
Tracy Finnegan

## Course Team Assistant

Yvonne Royals

## Authors

Saroj Datta
Ian Lyon
Bundy Mackintosh
Heather McLannahan
Kerry Murphy
Peter Naish
Daniel Nettle
Ignacio Romcro
Frederick Toates
Terry Whatson

## Multimedia

Sue Dugher
Spencer Harben
Will Rawes
Brian Richardson

## Other Contributors

Duncan Banks
Mike Stewart

## Consultant

Jose Julio Rodriguez Arellano

## Course Assessor

Philip Winn (University of St Andrews)

## Editors

Gerry Bearman
Rebecca Graham
Gillian Riley
Pamela Wardell

## Graphic Design

Steve Best
Sarah Hofton
Pam Owen

## Picture Researchers

Lydia K. Eaton
Deana Plummer

## Indexer

Jane Henley

**Cover image**: *Persistence of Memory* by Salvador Dali (Scala Picture Library)

# Contents

CHAPTER 1   LEARNING AND MEMORY   *Kerry Murphy and Peter Naish*   1

1.1   Introduction   1

1.2   Conditioning   5

1.3   The formation of links   12

1.4   Some complications   15

1.5   The declarative brain: in sickness and in health   18

1.6   The neurobiology of learning and memory   27

1.7   Hebbian synapses revealed: the hippocampus   30

1.8   The mechanics of a Hebbian synapse   34

1.9   Is LTP learning?   38

1.10  Memories that do not involve lasting synaptic modification: working memory revisited   42

1.11  Summary of Chapter 1   45

Learning outcomes for Chapter 1   46

Questions for Chapter 1   47

CHAPTER 2   FROM SOUND TO MEANING: HEARING, SPEECH AND LANGUAGE   *Daniel Nettle*   49

2.1   Introduction   49

2.2   The brain's task: the structure of language   50

2.3   The brain's solution: the machinery of language   64

2.4   Conclusions   77

Learning outcomes for Chapter 2   79

Questions for Chapter 2   80

ANSWERS TO QUESTIONS   82

REFERENCES AND FURTHER READING   86

ACKNOWLEDGEMENTS   88

INDEX   90

# LEARNING AND MEMORY

## 1.1 Introduction

Confronted with a chapter entitled 'learning and memory', in the context of an Open University course, you may well have a sinking feeling, as images of dreary revision and scary exams float through your mind! Even outside the exam situation, this subject area seems to get a bad press, with many of us complaining about how bad our memories are. In this chapter, we hope to convince you not only that our memories do what they have evolved to do remarkably well, but also that the whole topic of memory is far more fascinating and certainly less scary than you might have imagined. As you will discover, a good deal of the material to be addressed will concern the ways in which animals learn, but to get you thinking about the topic we will begin closer to home: with your own memory.

### 1.1.1 Forming and finding memories

Before starting to look at some of the details, it will be helpful to set the scene a little. In spite of the chapter title, the topic could just as well have been headed simply 'memory'. This term covers two processes: *storage* and *retrieval*. To have a memory, it is necessary that something is stored or, put another way, was learned. However, the storage is of little use unless it can be retrieved. When we complain of forgetting it may not be that we have lost any record of the item; it may be because the retrieval process has failed. In fact, an inability to recall a memory can result from three possible failures: unsuccessful storage, loss of the memory *trace* (analogous to fading ink), or failure to locate the trace at retrieval.

It will help you to get a feel for some of the retrieval processes if you try a few exercises. Because you are already 'involved', it would be even better if you gave them to someone else to do, without explaining the reason for doing them. For the first exercise, go through the following word list as quickly as possible, noting all the words in which the letter 'e' is used.

| | | | | |
|---|---|---|---|---|
| pepper | horse | table | squib | sleeve |
| zinc | saucer | chain | quay | bean |

Now, without looking back at those words (put your hand over them), try to remember as many of them as possible that contain the letter 'e'.

You probably didn't remember many, and that is hardly surprising, because although you must have seen the words clearly, you were not *attending* to their meaning. Memory has developed in such a way that it is more likely to store information to which we are attending: that is, material which is presumably important. Your lack of memory was a failure of storage.

For the following list, do not make any special effort to remember the words. Just work through them as quickly as possible, noting the number of words that are the names of birds.

| | | | | |
|---|---|---|---|---|
| blue tit | shark | swan | duck | snake |
| crow | eagle | lizard | spider | vulture |

Again, cover them and see how many you can remember that are the names of birds.

That time you probably did rather better – although not actively learning the word list, you had attended to the words in order to judge their category, and that generated a memory: this time storage was more successful.

For the final list, you should try to commit the words to memory, but do not spend long doing this. Just read through them once, reasonably quickly, and then carry out the instructions that follow.

| bed | night | pyjamas | dreaming | tired |
|-----|-------|---------|----------|-------|
| blankets | rest | dark | snoring | sheets |

This time, rather than just trying to remember the words, you can test yourself in a slightly different way. Below is another list of words, some of which are a repeat of those you have just read, while others are new. Your task is to identify the ones from the list above. Don't look back!

| radio | bed | dark | photograph | rest |
|-------|-----|------|------------|------|
| teapot | sleep | jacket | pyjamas | night |

I wonder whether you identified 'sleep' as being in the previous list? Many people do, although it was not actually there. You may well feel that the error was not surprising, given that the list had so many sleep-related words, but it is an error that reveals something about how our brains process information, and it helps to make a number of observations about the memory process.

The first thing you should note is that you did not learn the words in the sense that you might learn words in a foreign language. You already knew all the words, which means that they were already in your memory. As you read words like 'tired' and 'sheet' they *accessed* your memory, in a way that would possibly not have happened had you read 'cama', which is Spanish for bed. So, remembering in this context must have made a link with something already stored, and added to the information in some way, perhaps storing the fact that it was on this very page that the word was seen printed. It is probably true to say that, in almost all circumstances, additions to memories are made by linking to, or modifying material that is already stored.

Once information has been stored it appears to remain linked to related material. This is demonstrated by the fact that all the sleep-related words in the list must have acted through links to the memory's representation of 'sleep', so making the reader believe that they had seen that actual word. Just what we might mean by *representation* in memory, and how representations would be linked, are issues which will be considered later. However, it is worth mentioning at this stage that you would be right to guess that the links are formed through strengthening synapses.

## 1.1.2  Short-term and long-term memory

Our memory systems appear to store and act upon different kinds of information in different ways. For this reason it is helpful to subdivide the system into a number of different types.

A distinction that is commonly used is between *short-* and *long-term memory*. You may have heard people say something like 'I have quite a good short-term memory', meaning that they consider themselves good at remembering information for perhaps a few days. It is important to note that this is not the way the term is used by psychologists, although, just to confuse matters, neurobiologists do employ the short-term label more or less in this way. When psychologists refer to short-term memory they generally mean *really* short – just a few seconds! It is the sort of memory you would use to keep a telephone number in your head, until you reached the telephone to dial it. In fact it is an even poorer memory than the example might suggest because, as like as not, you would maintain that telephone number by *rehearsal*, that is by repeating it, over and over, until it was safely dialled. Without the repetition, the number would be lost from short-term memory very quickly. Contrast that with knowledge of say a friend's number, which you probably have stored safely away in long-term memory. Almost all the time it remains unnoticed, until you retrieve it to call the friend. Then, the number seems to come to the fore in some way, so that you can dial it, just like a number you have looked up and placed in short-term memory. It is as if short-term memory is not only a brief store for things that will not be needed again, but also somewhere to hold material retrieved from long-term memory. For this reason, psychologists prefer the term **working memory**, rather than short-term memory.

Short-term memory continues to be used as a label by neurobiologists however, but to mean something slightly different from that described so far. It is effectively long-term memory that is too new to have become well-established. The distinction becomes clearer if we consider what happens when a person is involved in an accident and receives a blow to the head. It is normal to suffer amnesia for the details of the accident. The amnesia is said to be *retrograde*, since it acts backwards in time from the moment of the accident. The amnesia will not normally be complete; an injured person remembers where they live, last year's summer holiday and so on, but would probably have forgotten everything about events that took place in the hours running up to the accident. Clearly, memory for this rather recent material is fragile in a way that really long-term memory is not. There is no clear dividing line between the two; sometimes the forgetting extends back only an hour or two, at other times it may cover days. The nature of the material to be remembered, the type of incident that resulted in forgetting, and also whether we are considering memory in humans or other animals, these all influence the apparent transition point from the insecure short-term memory to the really durable long-term memory. The physiological processes which underpin the transition will be discussed in a later section. For clarity, Figure 1.1 shows a scheme of the temporal categories of memory with which most neurobiologists and psychologists would agree and it is this scheme which will be used throughout the remainder of this chapter.

Returning to what is called working memory by psychologists, this really is the workhorse of our memory system. As an example of its use, try adding together (in your head) the numbers 27 and 18. When you have done the sum, try to decide where you accessed long-term memory (LTM) and where you used working memory.

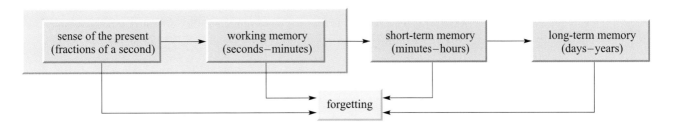

**Figure 1.1** The major temporal categories of human memory shown as a flow diagram. Note that for completeness a 'sense of the present' has been grouped with 'working memory'. An important feature of memory is that we also forget.

If your mental arithmetic is not too bad you should have found the answer 45. To do that you would have had to access your LTM, first to recognize the actual digits, then to recall various rules of addition. You probably started with the units, and retrieved the fact that $7 + 8 = 15$. Your working memory had to store the 5, and also remember that there would be a 1 to 'carry' (it was LTM that provided that rule). Back to LTM to remember that $2 + 1 = 3$, then use working memory to retrieve the carried 1, and make the answer 4. Finally, that earlier 5 must be picked up from working memory to obtain the complete 45. People who work with numbers a great deal may well have stored other results and techniques in their LTMs, enabling them to achieve the same result far more quickly. One of the reasons that practice improves many mental tasks is that it tends to 'lighten the load' for working memory by storing increasingly complex procedures in LTM.

### 1.1.3  Knowing *that* and knowing *how*

These two sorts of 'knowing' form another useful distinction in memory. Most of the memories discussed so far could be described as 'knowing that'. You know that 'bed' was in the word list, that $1 + 2 = 3$ and that London is the capital of England. This form of information storage is termed **declarative memory**, meaning that it is information that you could declare as a fact. However, a great deal of the information we have stored is linked to behaviour, rather than facts. It is the kind of information that enables us to speak, open a bottle, ride a bicycle or play the piano; it informs us how to do things, and is called **procedural memory**. It would often be very difficult to state these procedures in words, although we carry them out flawlessly. Take cycling as an example. You are probably aware that to stay upright it is necessary to steer in the direction that one is beginning to fall, but what about cornering? What is the first thing to do when you want to turn left, for example? You might think 'turn the handlebars to the left', but you would be wrong. By slowing down films of people cycling, it became possible to see that they first turned briefly in the 'wrong' direction: in our example, to the right. This causes the bicycle to start falling to the left. It is necessary to lean to the left when turning left, so this partial fall has to precede the actual turn.

Declarative memories, depending on their content, can be subdivided into two classes: **episodic memory** and **semantic memory**. Episodic memory refers to memory for past events in an individual's life. This system represents information concerning temporally dated episodes that can later be recollected. Episodic memory stores the cumulated events of one's life, an individual's autobiography. Semantic memory refers to knowledge about the world. This form of memory contains organized information such as facts, concepts and vocabulary. The content of semantic memory is explicitly known and available for recall. Unlike episodic memory, however, semantic memory has no necessary temporal landmarks. It does not refer to particular events in a person's past. A simple illustration of this difference is that one may recall the difference between episodic and semantic memory, or one may recall the encounter when the difference was first explained.

◆ What type of declarative memory is involved in the memory that 'Mars is the fourth planet in the Solar System'?

◆ The information recalled here is a fact, and this is an example of semantic memory.

◆ What type of declarative memory is used to allow an individual to declare that 'yesterday, my alarm clock failed to ring and I was late for work'?

◆ This is an autobiographical statement and requires the use of episodic memory.

Acquiring declarative memories may need only a single presentation of the fact: you may still remember that 'cama' is Spanish for bed. However, procedural memories are generally acquired more slowly, through a process of trial and error (and frequent tumbles from the bike!). Clearly, animals cannot 'declare', and anyone who has trained a horse, or taught a dog tricks, will be aware that it is a process of trial and error. This is important, because a great deal of basic research into memory processes has been undertaken using animals, a far harder task for the experimenter than teaching people lists of words. In the sections that follow there will be many references to animal learning. You may wonder why we do not continue exclusively in this chapter with human memory, but it is worth recognizing that we are a very special case. Millennia of evolution have equipped animals with a means for learning to produce appropriate behaviour in changing situations. We too have inherited those mechanisms, but to some extent they have been submerged beneath our abilities for language (see Chapter 2) and complex thought. This chapter is concerned with the basic processes that are common to all animals with reasonably advanced nervous systems.

## Summary of Section 1.1

Memories tend to be formed for material to which attention is being paid. The formation of memories is a process of modification and linking, involving neural synapses. Before material becomes well-established in long-term memory, there is a relatively short period of vulnerability, called short-term memory by neurobiologists. Humans have a 'working memory', in which they can manipulate some kinds of information, reflect upon it and express it in speech. Both humans and other animals can store information which will guide their behaviour (procedural memory). Even in humans, it may be impossible to verbalize the contents of these memories.

# 1.2   Conditioning

Humans have been involved in training animals for thousands of years, but the first scientific study of animal learning was carried out by a Russian physiologist, working at the end of the 19th century and in the early years of the 20th century. His name was Ivan Pavlov and it is a measure of the importance of his work that the phrase, 'Pavlov and his dogs', has become so well-known. The kind of learning that he demonstrated was termed *conditioning* (for reasons that will be explained); it turns out that there is more than one type of conditioning so, since Pavlov's was the first to be described, it is referred to as *classical* conditioning. An alternative label, naturally enough, is *Pavlovian* conditioning.

## 1.2.1   Classical conditioning

As an aid to swallowing and digestion, dogs produce copious quantities of saliva. Salivation is a reflex response to the presentation of food. Clearly then there must be links between sensory neurons that detect the presence of food, and neurons that stimulate the secretion of saliva. Although we have seen that memories are represented as links, salivation is not a memory: it is, as we have just noted, a reflex.

The animal is born with this automatic response and does not have to learn it. Pavlov was investigating the nature of the reflex and measuring the quantity of saliva produced, when his experiments were rather disrupted by the dogs beginning to salivate at the 'wrong' time! They started to produce saliva when they saw that he was about to bring food. Pavlov did not ignore this chance observation, he investigated it, and achieved fame.

For his investigation, Pavlov began by confirming that the sound of a bell would not stimulate a dog to produce saliva. Next, he rang a bell just as food was placed in the dog's mouth, and each subsequent time that the dog was fed. Finally, he rang the bell without giving the food – this time the sound of the bell did lead to salivation. The sequence of events is illustrated in Figure 1.2.

**Figure 1.2** Pavlovian conditioning in dogs – cartoon illustrating the key points of Pavlov's ground-breaking experiment. A dog's normal response when presented with food is to salivate (a), whereas the sound of a bell does not normally elicit a response (b). By repeatedly pairing the presentation of food with the sound of a bell (c), it is possible to alter the dog's response to the bell, so that, after conditioning, the sound of the bell alone triggers salivation (d) – the bell has become an anticipatory cue for the presentation of food.

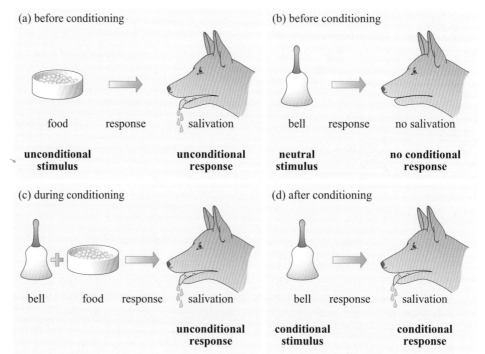

Many of us have become so familiar with Pavlov's experiment that it tends to be taken for granted, but it is, in fact, quite startling. Food produces the salivation response automatically; the link has developed through evolution. The sound of a bell has no relevance to food and is not even a 'natural' component of a dog's environment. Nevertheless, neurons activated by that sound must have formed links with those involved in the automatic salivation response. How might that occur? Those of us with pets, who tend to be rather anthropomorphic about them (i.e. suppose them to have human qualities and abilities), might imagine the dog hearing the bell and thinking, 'Ah, dinner's coming!' Well, although Fido is unlikely to think in words, it is conceivable that the bell would evoke a memory of food, which in turn might lead to salivation. So, the question we are trying to address is whether the salivation is directly triggered, or whether it is mediated by a memory of some kind, such as a visual image. A human experiment can suggest an answer to this.

Like other animals, we have a number of reflexes. One that is easily observed is the eye-blink. We automatically blink our eyes if they are touched, or if something moves quickly towards them. For experimental purposes, a puff of air directed at the eyes is an effective stimulus; it is non-injurious, but reliably makes a person blink. In the light of the Pavlov story, you will not be surprised to know that if a buzzer sounds each time there is an air puff, it does not take long for the buzzer alone to make the person blink. Unlike dogs, the experimental subjects are able to discuss the experience, and they state that they do not experience *conscious* thoughts such as, 'Here comes another air puff'. The blink is automatic and is not preceded by any conscious imagery or expectation. We might presume this to be the case for the salivating dog also; classical conditioning is an automatic process that links a new stimulus to an existing reflex behaviour.

This interpretation was believed for a long time, and it will serve for now, to set the scene. This subject will be revisited in Section 1.2.5. Notice, however, that the suggested conclusion concerning the dog was derived from asking humans about something similar. We have already seen, in the context of cycling, that humans are not always able to give accurate accounts of their behaviour, so it would be unwise to draw very strong conclusions here. We will have to return later to the issue of whether something akin to thinking might be involved in classical conditioning, because, as is so often the case, things are not as simple as they seem!

## 1.2.2   The nomenclature of conditioning

We hope that you will have found the description of learning a new link to an old behaviour reasonably straightforward. Unfortunately, the technical terms used to describe the different stimuli and responses are not so obvious and that is why we have avoided using them. However, you will meet them elsewhere so they need to be mastered – this task is complicated by the existence of alternative forms for some of these terms.

- A dog that salivates at the sound of a bell has been changed: it has been *conditioned*. As you have already discovered, the process is called conditioning.

- Before conditioning, the dog would salivate to the usual stimulus – food in the mouth. Since conditioning is not required to produce this response, the food is called the **unconditional stimulus** and the salivation the **unconditional response** (Figure 1.2a). (Sometimes, instead of 'unconditional', the term *unconditioned* is used. Food is an unconditional stimulus for salivation, in the sense that saliva appears unconditionally – it is automatic.)

- Before conditioning, the sound of the bell has no effect, so it is termed a **neutral stimulus** (Figure 1.2b).

- After conditioning, the bell becomes a **conditional stimulus**. Salivation to the sound of the bell is the result of conditioning, so it is termed the **conditional response** (Figure 1.2d).

- Since the sound of the bell and food are presented in association, this type of conditioning is an example of an associative link – indeed, Pavlovian conditioning is often referred to as *associative* conditioning.

These rather long terms are often abbreviated. Thus the unconditional stimulus is the UCS and the conditional stimulus the CS.

Obviously, the various terms are not reserved for food and saliva; they are applied to any relevant components of a classical conditioning scenario. You should try to apply them to the human eye-blink effect.

◆   What are the appropriate terms for the eye-blink, the air puff and the buzzer? Do these change as the animal becomes conditioned?

◆   The blink is an unconditional response (to the air puff). The air puff is an unconditional stimulus. The buzzer is a neutral stimulus. After the conditioning process has taken place, the buzzer is termed the conditional stimulus and the blink given in response to the buzzer is the conditional response.

### 1.2.3   Instrumental conditioning

So far we have referred, somewhat vaguely, to the formation of links. It will be necessary to explore that concept a little more closely, but first we will deal with another form of conditioning; it is called *instrumental conditioning* and involves *rewards* or *punishments*. This conditioning is what we normally associate with animal training. Incidentally, it is strange that Pavlovian conditioning was researched first, because it must generally be rare for an animal's behaviour to become linked to a hitherto irrelevant stimulus. On the other hand, learning how to gain a reward (food, say) is an everyday event for many animals. We employ this kind of learning, instrumental conditioning, when we teach a dog to perform tricks. A reward (a biscuit, pat on the head, etc.) is available to the dog but the reward is given only when the dog produces the desired behaviour. Thus, the dog is *instrumental* in obtaining the reward. The dog is in effect in control, in a way that it is not when exposed to the ringing of the bell and its own reflex behaviour. This is another form of associative learning, in this case it relies on behaviour being associated with a consequence such as food. Punishment occurs where a noxious stimulus follows a response and the frequency of showing that response thereby declines. For example, a rat moving into part of its cage might trigger a loud sound. The efficacy of this as a 'punishment' would be indexed by a reduction in the time spent in the offending part of the cage.

We sometimes seek quite complex behaviour from an animal, a sequence of actions that it is unlikely to stumble upon by chance. Training in these circumstances generally involves rewarding a series of approximations to the desired behaviour. When the animal begins to master one step, the reward is withheld until the next step is performed. This gradual 'moulding' of the behaviour is termed *shaping*.

Teaching a dog to perform tricks is a little more complex than has been suggested, because the dog is usually required to also learn a command from its owner, that is associated with the behaviour and subsequent reward. Laboratory-based research employs basic instrumental conditioning and the animal most frequently used is the rat. A great deal of research has been conducted using a Skinner box (Book 1, Section 1.4.2). You will recall that, typically, when the rat presses a lever, this action causes the release of a food pellet, and so rewards the behaviour. Lever-pressing is an example of a behaviour that a rat might take some time to discover. So, shaping is often used initially, first giving the rat food when it enters the section of the box where the lever is located, and then when it approaches the lever, and so on. Eventually, the rat becomes conditioned to press the lever when it wants food. The delivery of food is said to *reinforce* the behaviour, that is, to make it more likely to be performed in the future. The convenience of the Skinner box is that the lever-pressing can be logged automatically, so that the rat's rate of pressing can be monitored over long periods without the experimenter being present (Figure 1.3).

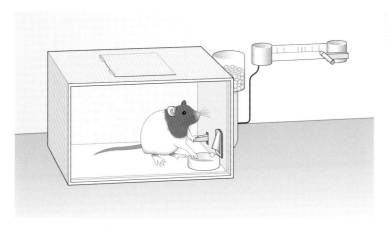

**Figure 1.3**  A Skinner box set up so that the number of lever presses a rat makes can be logged.

## 1.2.4  Stimulus–response, or something more?

In the context of the classical conditioning of dogs, we considered briefly whether the bell–food–saliva link might contain some intermediate mental event, or even conscious awareness. We concluded there was probably no such step in the sequence. It is pertinent to ask a similar question here; in other words, is what the rat has learned in the nature of a procedural memory or does it have something of the 'declarative' about it? Since it is a behavioural sequence that is produced, one might conclude that the stored information guiding the behaviour was simply procedural (like riding a bicycle). The internal stimulus of hunger would initiate this behaviour automatically, giving rise directly to the response of pressing the lever.

Skinner believed that there is nothing more taking place in a rat's brain other than a simple sequence much as described above. Psychologists who subscribed to this kind of belief were termed *behaviourists*, and theories suggesting a direct stimulus–response (S–R) link were labelled *S–R theories*. Behaviourists denied the need to appeal to any kind of 'mental event'; behaviour was all that could be observed and, therefore, was all that should be used in devising an account of what was going on. (Note, however, that Skinner did not subscribe to this exact sequence.) Nevertheless, it is logically possible that an alternative to the S–R sequence could be taking place. Intuitively, the rat's pressing of a lever is less automatic than an in-built reflex; the animal might for example be distracted, so that, although hungry, it would not press the lever. It seems conceivable that the stimulus of hunger would trigger something more akin to a declarative memory. Although the rat could not declare its memory as a human could, there may be a sense in which it *knew that* pressing the bar would produce food. It might, for example, have some kind of mental image of the process. Such an idea was too fanciful for the behaviourists, but another type of experiment can cast light on the issue.

Lever-pressing is a very immediate way of obtaining food. In another class of experiments the rat needs to produce a more protracted sequence of steps in order to receive the reward/food. A hungry rat is released on one side of a maze and some food awaits it on the other side (Figure 1.4a). It is natural for rats to explore their surroundings, so it eventually discovers the food; the time taken to do so is recorded. The rat is then placed at the start once more, and again the time to reach the food is noted. If this sequence is repeated, the time is gradually reduced; the rat learns to avoid dead-ends and to ignore possible, but longer routes. The rat has been conditioned to take the shortest route (Figure 1.4b).

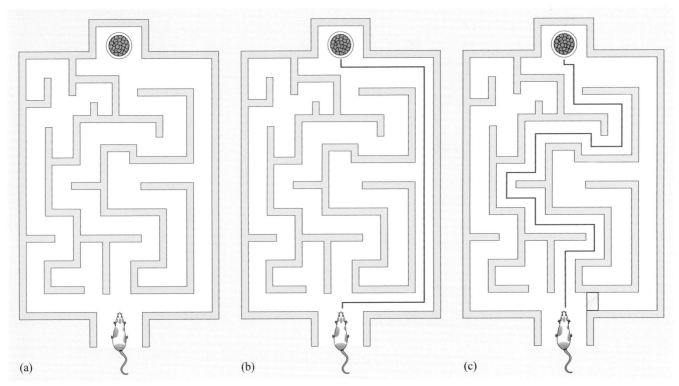

**Figure 1.4**   A maze with more than one solution. First look at (a) and decide which is the shortest route to the food reward. As in humans, a rat will always find the quickest route to the reward (b). If the shortest route is denied to the rat by a barrier, the rat will now take the only other route available (c).

◆   What kind of conditioning has the rat experienced?

◆   Instrumental conditioning.

In S–R terms, the stimulus to set out through the maze is the hunger, the response is to take the best route, and the link between the two was reinforced by the reward of food. Notice that, according to this theory, other potential responses are not rewarded and so will not be elicited by the stimulus. However, there is more to come!

In the next stage, once the rat has learned its route well (Figure 1.4b), a barrier is placed across the favoured path. In response, the rat makes its way back to the less-favoured but still viable route, so still reaches its food relatively quickly (see Figure 1.4c). This route had received little reinforcement before, so why did the rat take it? It has been suggested that, during the early exploratory phase of these experiments, a rat develops a *cognitive map* of the maze. Finding itself thwarted on the shortest route, the animal is able to consult its mental map and choose an alternative path. There seem to be more steps here than in a simple S–R sequence, in fact it sounds very much as if the rat 'knows that' there are many paths, with food at the end of one of them.

### 1.2.5   Classical conditioning re-examined

Having just concluded from instrumental conditioning that an animal such as a rat can in some way 'know that', it is worth reconsidering the processes of classical conditioning, where we concluded that an animal seems to 'know' nothing. You may remember that we ended Section 1.2.1 with the warning that things were not as simple as they seemed. In some ways that is unfortunate, because, as you will discover in Section 1.3, the straightforward account of classical conditioning given earlier is quite easy to explain on the basis of simple changes in synapses. However, scientific theories generally advance when cases are found that cannot be properly explained by the current theory; we are about to look at two such cases.

It became clear, even to Pavlov, that there was more going on than was implied by the simple concept of conditioning a reflex. He observed that his dogs would come running to be fed, when they heard the bell. The running was not an automatic reflex, so this sounds more like an example of what was later to be known as instrumental conditioning.

One of Pavlov's pupils went on to devise an ingenious, if bizarre experiment. He used a sheep, placing it so that it stood with one hoof on a metal plate. Whenever a bell sounded a small electrical current was passed through the plate, giving the sheep an electric shock. It naturally lifted its leg, and soon learned to do so to the sound of the bell alone. The leg-raising response to the bell is another example of classical conditioning and in this instance indicates that something more than simple reflex processing has occurred.

◈   What are the appropriate labels for the stimulus and response in this case?

◆   The shock is the unconditional stimulus. The bell starts as a neutral stimulus, but becomes the conditional stimulus. Leg-raising becomes the conditional response.

That is only half the story, but I will digress for a moment. A more cruel version of the procedure was used to train the dancing bears of the Middle Ages. During training, every time the music started a hot metal plate was pushed forward, under the unfortunate animal's forepaws. This caused it to rear onto its hind legs, and it learned to do so whenever the music played, so producing the semblance of dancing.

To return to the sheep, the next phase of the experiment was the part that we are sure you will long remember! The poor animal was suspended upside down, now with its head touching the metal plate. The big question was: 'What would it do to the sound of a bell?' Simple conditioning would predict that it would needlessly, but automatically, jerk its leg. The actual result was far more interesting: the sheep raised its head away from the plate. It had learned to associate the bell with a shock arising from the metal. It is hard to see this as anything but an example of 'knowing that'.

As a consequence of observations and experiments like these, it is now considered that conditioning of both kinds is best described as a process of learning that 'Event B generally follows Event A'. If Event A is the sound of a bell and Event B is the arrival of food, then a dog may actually be producing saliva in response to the anticipation of B, rather than as a direct response to A. In the case of instrumental conditioning, event A is the animal's own behaviour. Note, however, 'anticipation' need not require conscious awareness.

## Summary of Section 1.2

Behaviour can be conditioned to be triggered by a neutral stimulus if the cause of the behaviour and the neutral stimulus have been paired repeatedly and occurred close together in time.

Classical conditioning involves behaviour that is produced in response to an unconditional stimulus. A neutral stimulus is then paired closely with the unconditional stimulus. As a result, the previously neutral stimulus becomes conditioned, and often elicits the same response as the unconditional stimulus.

Instrumental conditioning occurs when behaviour is rewarded. The behaviour becomes reinforced, making it more likely to be repeated in future. An alternative is to use punishment, where the learned behaviour is instrumental in avoiding the punishment.

Instrumental conditioning in animals may be mediated by stored information analogous to human declarative memories.

Classical conditioning was thought to produce direct stimulus–response links, with no evidence for any associated mental events. However, evidence suggests that the process may be more sophisticated, involving learning that one event follows another.

# 1.3   The formation of links

The human brain has been estimated to contain up to one hundred billion neurons. Each of these may have synaptic links with a thousand or more of the other neurons (Book 4, Section 1.4.1). Not surprisingly, the brain has been described as 'massively interconnected'. Although smaller brains, such as that of a rat, contain fewer neurons, the interconnectedness of the structure remains a key feature – it is this characteristic that makes learning possible. To show how this is possible, we will consider a very simple example: classical conditioning. The account will assume that this conditioning consists solely of the formation of links to automatic, reflex responses. At the end of the description we will look briefly at more complex processes.

## 1.3.1   Hebbian learning

All forms of information storage require that a storage medium is modified in some way. For example, written notes place lines of dark ink on the pristine paper while video-recordings disturb the ordered arrangement of the magnetization in the video tape. In the brain the storage medium is the great web of connections. Note, a neuron itself is not actually a storage element, it is the synapses made between the pre- and postsynaptic neurons which are liable to alteration and hence provide the mechanism for learning.

The mechanisms by which synapses change will be described in more detail in later sections of this chapter; at this point we will just consider the basic principles. They are surprisingly simple, and were first proposed by the psychologist Donald Hebb in 1949, long before the physiology was understood. You will recall (Book 1, Section 2.4.3 and Book 4, Chapter 1) that a synapse is the link between two neurons, referred to as the pre- and postsynaptic neurons. When an action potential in the presynaptic neuron reaches the synapse it causes the release of neurotransmitter. This in turn influences the postsynaptic neuron, and may contribute to an action potential in that neuron also (i.e. it may fire). Hebb suggested that if the postsynaptic neuron fired when the presynaptic terminal was releasing transmitter, then the ability of the presynaptic neuron to influence the postsynaptic neuron on subsequent occasions would be increased. In other words, the synapse is modified in some way that increases what is termed the *synaptic efficiency*. Intuitively this change in a synapse is plausible, and might be seen as underpinning the observation that 'practice makes perfect'. On every occasion that activity in the presynaptic neuron was accompanied by firing in the postsynaptic cell, the synapse would become a little more effective, so that it could be described as learning the link between the two neurons. The modification is referred to as *Hebbian learning* and a synapse that behaves like this as a *Hebbian synapse*.

## 1.3.2  The role of Hebbian synapses in classical conditioning

From the preceding section it should be clear that gradual increases in synaptic efficiency would strengthen the link between two neurons, so that one would become better able to influence the other. What may not be immediately obvious however, is how a completely non-influential neuron could come to have any influence on another. To be specific, how would a neuron that becomes active during the ringing of a bell ever develop any influence over a neuron that controls salivation? On the face of it, the account in Section 1.3.1 seems to be saying that synapses can only grow in efficiency if they are somewhat effective in the first place. However, Pavlov showed that normally the ring of a bell is not at all effective in causing a dog to produce saliva.

There are two elements to the explanation of this apparent puzzle. The first is concealed in the wording of the preceding section. It stated that synaptic efficiency would increase if the postsynaptic neuron fired *while* the presynaptic cell was releasing transmitter. This is not the same as saying that transmitter from the presynaptic neuron was the *cause* of postsynaptic firing. It may indeed have been so, but the strengthening of the synapse would take place just as effectively if the two neurons merely happened to be active at the same time. The second point to recall is that brains are massively interconnected; there will inevitably be a few neurons that become active to the sound of the bell, which just happen also to form synapses with neurons whose activities cause salivation. These synapses will be few and inefficient, so the sound of a bell could not be expected to initiate salivation – at least, not until after conditioning.

To complete the explanation, we need an abbreviation for a neuron that is activated by the bell; since the bell starts as a neutral stimulus, we will call this neuron the *neutral* neuron. In reality there would be very large numbers of neurons and synapses involved, but for simplicity we will consider just three as illustrated in Figure 1.5.

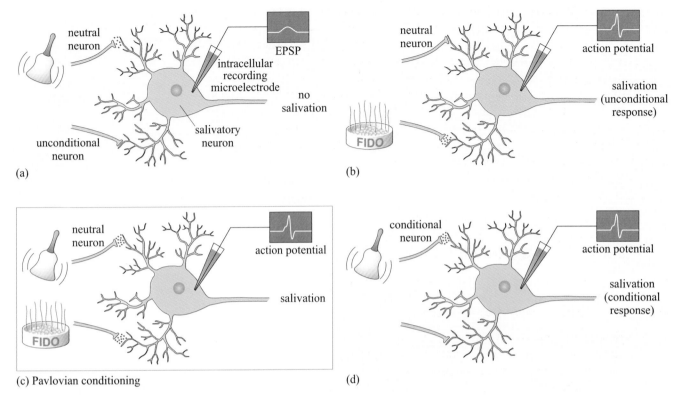

**Figure 1.5**  A stylized cartoon showing the convergence of both an auditory input (the neutral neuron) and the input activated by the presentation of food (the unconditional neuron) that initiates salivation (the salivatory neuron). (a) Activation of the neutral neuron by the ringing of the bell fails to generate an action potential in the salivatory neuron. (b) Activation of the unconditional neuron by the presentation of food generates an action potential in the salivatory neuron – causing salivation. (c) Pavlovian conditioning: the auditory input is activated at the same time food is presented. As in (b), an action potential is elicited in the salivatory neuron. (d) As a consequence of conditioning, the efficacy of the auditory input has been enhanced so that the ringing of the bell alone is sufficient to elicit an action potential in the salivatory neuron and thus initiate salivation.

Initially, as indicated, the link between the neutral neuron and the postsynaptic cell is very weak. Consequently, release of neurotransmitter by the neutral neuron is unlikely to cause the postsynaptic neuron to fire so that it never results in the release of saliva (Figure 1.5a). In contrast, the presynaptic neuron that responds to the presentation of food, does have an efficient synapse with the postsynaptic neuron; so it reliably causes firing in the latter, and hence salivation (Figure 1.5b). If we now recreate the conditions of Pavlov's experiments, by activating the presynaptic neurons that represent the 'bell' and the 'presentation' of food, so that whenever the neutral neuron is active the postsynaptic neuron is firing, then the previously weak synapse will gradually strengthen (Figure 1.5c). Eventually this synapse will have sufficient efficiency to trigger firing in the postsynaptic neuron, without the help of the presynaptic neuron that responds to food (Figure 1.5d).

◆ Draw a diagram and label the presynaptic neurons (one of which is the neutral neuron), postsynaptic neuron and neutral neuron to identify the elements involved in the conditioning of an eye-blink to a buzzer. (The unconditional stimulus is a puff of air.)

◆ One of the presynaptic neurons represents a neuron affected by the puff of air. The postsynaptic neuron is a neuron that synapses with muscles in the eyelid, to cause blinking. The neutral neuron is a particular presynaptic neuron that fires to the sound of a buzzer.

We suggested earlier (Section 1.2.5) that, at least in some cases, classical conditioning probably involves learning that one event will follow another. That sounds a more complex link than has just been described. In fact the principles are very similar. For example, there must be a certain set of neurons that fire whenever a dog receives food. It would be as easy for 'bell neurons' to form strong synapses with these as it would be for them to do so with 'saliva neurons'. Repeated activity in both the bell and food neurons would strengthen the synapses, so that eventually the bell alone would produce activity that was rather similar to that normally produced by food. Consequently, the sound of the bell would, in some sense, 'bring food to mind' for the dog, hence initiating salivation.

## Summary of Section 1.3

Learning is mediated by the modification of the efficiency of synapses in the brain. A more efficient synapse implies that activity in a presynaptic neuron is more likely to lead to firing in the postsynaptic neuron.

A synapse grows in efficiency when the postsynaptic neuron reliably fires at the same time as the presynaptic neuron is releasing transmitter substance. The increase in efficiency is called Hebbian learning.

The simplest model of classical conditioning utilizes three sets of neurons. The first two sets are associated with the unconditioned stimulus and response (e.g. food and saliva) and they have existing strong synapses. The third set of neurons is activated by the neutral stimulus (e.g. a bell). Initially these have weak synapses with the response neurons but Hebbian learning increases their efficiency.

# 1.4   Some complications

There is general acceptance amongst scientists that memories reside in the patterns of synaptic strengths within networks of neurons. However, there is a large jump in complexity from the processes which are presumed to underpin classical conditioning, to your ability to store the information that a list at the start of this chapter did not contain the word 'sleep' (Section 1.1.1). Before looking at the biochemistry of synaptic change, we will briefly consider some of the more complex aspects of memory.

## 1.4.1   Learning in instrumental conditioning

In Section 1.2.4, we saw that instrumental conditioning may imply a more elaborate kind of information storage than is required for classical conditioning. This complexity becomes obvious when one tries to construct a simple Hebbian learning account of what takes place. Consider a conditioned rat, scampering though the maze towards the reward that awaits it at the end. What active neurons initiated this behaviour? Presumably those which, for simplicity, we will call 'hunger' neurons. The rat would be less motivated to run if it were not hungry. However, maze-running is not a natural response to hunger, so before conditioning there would have been no effective synaptic links between hunger neurons and the specific behaviour that takes the rat along the correct route to the food. It could be argued that hunger would at least initiate explorative and food-searching behaviour such as going through the maze. However, consider another example: a dog that has learned to 'shake hands'. When its owner issues the command the dog sits down and raises one front paw. Paw-lifting is most certainly not a natural response to human speech in dogs! Hebbian learning would require that another set of synapses was driving the behaviour and, because the owner always said 'shake hands' at that moment, the 'human voice' neurons would become gradually more efficient at triggering the behaviour. The problem for this explanation is that the behaviour is effectively 'unnatural', so there should not be any existing neural pathways that could cause the dog to go through the routine.

Clearly the reward element is important in instrumental conditioning; the dog will not learn to shake hands if it is not suitably rewarded during training. Furthermore, the reward has to be more or less instantaneous; the dog does not learn if the reward is delayed. This reminds us that synapses will be strengthened only if both the pre- and the postsynaptic neurons are simultaneously active. If the time between triggering the behaviour and receiving the reward is sufficiently brief, it is conceivable that the 'triggering' neurons would still be active. However, it seems unlikely that the 'human voice' neurons in the dog would still be active by the time the animal had sat down and raised its paw. Similarly, the rat will have a long sequence of twists and turns to negotiate before reaching its reward.

It is possible that in the early stages of learning, it is the very last element of the behaviour that is involved in the Hebbian learning. Thus, 'reward' neurons might fire while there was still activity in the neurons that directed the rat round the last corner of the maze. On a subsequent run, as the rat approached and recognized the last corner, there would be activity in the appropriate neurons that, through the previous learning, would trigger the reward neurons. This explanation supposes that the rat experiences a feeling of reward *before* the real reward is reached. As a result, the rat might gradually experience the anticipatory gratification at increasingly early stages on the route. In effect, to venture into the maze would acquire something of the reward value of actual eating, so a hungry rat would naturally start to engage in that behaviour. If you recall that conditioning probably involves learning that Event B tends to follow Event A, then it is indeed possible that the rat genuinely anticipates the outcome of its actions.

For the dog a similar explanation may be applicable. The dog's behaviour is likely to be shaped by the owner, first rewarding sitting down and then rewarding any tendency to lift one paw. This would be equivalent to putting the rat's reward at increasingly greater distances from the start of the maze. Again, an anticipatory sense of reward might be predicted and this would strengthen associated synapses.

You will not need to be told that this was a complicated story! To refer to anticipation sounds rather like 'knowing that' and we have already pointed out that a rat appears to develop a mental map of a maze. If we are prepared to accept the possibility that a rat may in some way learn the layout of a maze without needing the external reinforcement of food, then we can to some extent side-step the complications of this section. We can say, simply, that hunger activates the knowledge that there is food in a particular location and the rat goes to collect it. This would not have been the kind of explanation favoured by the behaviourists!

## 1.4.2  Learning, timing and repetition

The simple Hebbian account explains that new effective links are formed when previously unassociated neurons fire simultaneously, and on several occasions. Thus, the bell and food have to be presented together (not at different times) and the pairing has to be repeated for conditioning to take place. This makes sense from an evolutionary viewpoint because events may sometimes occur together by chance, but an animal should not learn to associate any such spurious connections. Only if events are reliably and repeatedly paired is it likely that they are causally linked and therefore worth learning.

There is a striking exception to the above rule; it has been named the *Garcia effect* after the psychologist who discovered it. The Garcia effect concerns the impact of gastro-intestinal illness upon food preference. It would clearly be advantageous to an animal if, having eaten injurious food-stuff and become ill, it learned to avoid the food in future. There are two difficulties here. First, repeated pairing of food and illness is likely to have fatal rather than Hebbian results! The second problem is that an animal is not likely to experience the symptoms of poisoning until some time after ingesting the food, so the other rule for Hebbian learning appears to have been broken. Nevertheless, animals clearly do learn to avoid substances associated with illness. In Garcia's experiment, rats were given saccharine-flavoured water to drink; rats like the sweet taste. Some hours later, the rats were injected with a substance to induce nausea. Finally, when they had recovered they were presented again with the saccharine solution. Although they had been only one pairing of the taste and the nausea, and although the two were widely separated in time, the rats rejected the solution. Further research showed that it was specifically the taste that the rats had learned to avoid, and that the learning was most effective if the nausea followed a novel taste experience, rather than a taste with which the rat was familiar (where there had been no previous illness).

The Garcia effect can also be observed in humans. Patients undergoing chemo- or radiotherapy generally suffer from nausea immediately following a treatment session. Many report forming a strong dislike for foods that they may have eaten before attending a session. This is a powerful effect because, unlike the rat, the human is aware that the feelings of sickness are not linked to the food. Nevertheless, rather in the manner of a phobia, the intellectual awareness of the true nature of the situation is insufficient to overcome the automatic response. The evolutionary advantages of the Garcia effect are clear, but the underlying mechanisms that make this kind of learning possible are not understood.

Nearly all mammals that have been tested have shown a Garcia effect, but an interesting exception is the vampire bat. These animals feed on blood (generally from cattle). Their only source of food is inevitably fresh and uncontaminated, so there is no evolutionary pressures to learn any form of avoidance behaviour. In fact, if they were ever to avoid their food source, then they would die anyway, since this is the only type of food that vampire bats consume.

### 1.4.3 Preparedness and phobias

The ease with which very specific links are formed between stomach upset and previously ingested food is a case of what is termed *preparedness*. We are prepared to learn these links more easily than other kinds of association, presumably having special instinctual mechanisms in place to do so.

It has been suggested that some phobias are also examples of preparedness and that they too are the adaptive results of evolution. People can sometimes develop phobias for all kinds of objects or situations, but the most common cases are for creatures such as spiders (arachnophobia) or snakes (ophidiophobia), and for heights (acrophobia). During an early period of human evolution (believed to have taken place largely in Africa) spiders, scorpions and snakes would have been a potential danger to our ancestors, as would the possibility of falling from a height (our early ancestors are believed to have been tree-dwellers). A preparedness to learn to avoid such things would have clear survival value, and our ancestors who did have this propensity would be more likely to live long enough to pass on their genes. Our propensity to develop these fears is so high that the phobias are generally acquired without needing to experience a bite or sting for example.

In Britain one is far more likely to be killed by a London bus than by a spider bite, yet while arachnophobia abounds, few people develop 'bus phobia'; there were no buses mowing down our African ancestors! As with the Garcia effect, phobias are frustratingly resistant to logic and intellectualization.

### Summary of Section 1.4

Some forms of learning appear to involve more than the simple processes of adjusting the efficiency of a Hebbian synapse, although ultimately they must result in some kind of synaptic modification.

Instrumental conditioning is an example of learning that cannot be explained as simply as classical conditioning. It is necessary to propose that a series of steps becomes conditioned, or that the conditioned animal acquires something like a declarative memory that holds the anticipation of a reward.

Learning to avoid a novel foodstuff when it is followed by a period of nausea appears to be a special case of conditioning. It is called the Garcia effect and requires neither repetition nor simultaneous experience of the taste and the nausea to form the link. The response is an example of so-called preparedness.

Many phobias may also be examples of preparedness, i.e. adaptations that facilitate the acquisition of an avoidance response to objects or situations that would have been injurious to our ancestors.

## 1.5    The declarative brain: in sickness and in health

### 1.5.1    H.M. revisited

So far we have discussed how animals were used by scientists such as Pavlov, and psychologists such as Skinner, to study and define the different forms of learning. From such experiments, it should be possible for you to infer something about brain function. At this stage of your reading, the link between Pavlov's dogs and the model of synaptic strengthening postulated by Hebb should hopefully be apparent. However, to further our understanding, it still remains necessary to 'open' the brain and ask what is happening at the level of different brain regions, of neurons and importantly, at the level of the synapses that participate in learning and memory.

The first description of the anatomical distinction between declarative and procedural memory was revealed by the amazing case of H.M. We first met H.M. in Book 1 (Section 1.1.5). You may recall that, in an attempt to cure his epilepsy, surgeons made a bilateral excision of the medial temporal lobe, including the hippocampus. The surgery cured his epilepsy but left him with a lasting memory and cognitive impairment. The importance of H.M. was that originally it was assumed that damage to the medial temporal lobe would affect all forms of memory equally. However, the pattern of deficit found in H.M. clearly showed that this was not the case. He was no

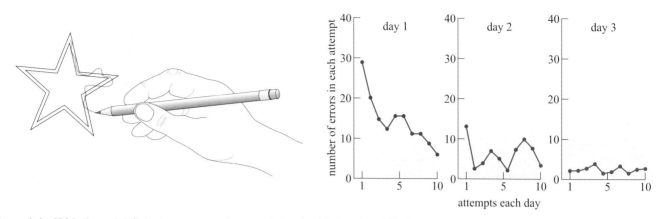

**Figure 1.6** H.M. showed definite improvement in any task involved in learning skilled movements. One such skilled task was tracing between two outlines of a star while viewing his hand in a mirror – why don't you have a go at this at home? The graphs plot the number of times, in each trial, that he strayed outside the outlines as he drew the star.

longer able to form new declarative memories, and both semantic and episodic memory systems were impaired. However, and importantly, declarative memories formed prior to surgery were largely spared. Crucially, H.M. still retained the ability to learn new motor skills (procedural memory) at a normal rate. For example, he learned to draw the outline of a star while looking at his hand and the star in a mirror (Figure 1.6). Like normal participants learning this task, H.M. initially made many mistakes, but after several days of training his performance was error-free and indistinguishable from that of normal subjects. However, unlike normal participants, H.M. had no recollection of 'learning' the task.

◈ Why did H.M. fail to remember that he had learnt the procedural skill of mirror drawing?

◆ Whilst H.M. could learn new procedural (knowing 'how') tasks, because of his impairment in declarative memory (knowing 'that') he was unable to recall having learnt the task.

Study of patients with lesions restricted to the hippocampus, leaving all the cerebral cortex intact, has shed light on the role of higher brain centres in the formation and long-term storage of memory. It appears that the hippocampus is not the site of long-term memory, but mediates the initial steps of long-term memory. The memory is first formed in the hippocampus and then over the course of several days is slowly transferred into the *cerebral cortical storage system*. The relatively slow addition of information to the cortex permits new information to be stored in a way that does not disrupt existing memories. Damage to the cortex, in particular the association cortex, has a direct effect on the recall or processing of declarative memory. Patients with a lesion in the association areas have difficulty in recognizing faces, objects and places in their familiar world. Indeed, lesions in different association areas give rise to specific defects in either semantic or episodic memory. Figure 1.7 shows the results of a simple experiment where two patients suffering from cortical lesions were asked to draw and to name verbally a set of images or drawings. Patient A is able to copy the drawings accurately but is unable to name them, demonstrating a cognitive impairment called *associative agnosia*. Patient B, suffering from an impairment called *apperceptive agnosia*, is unable to reproduce even the simplest of drawings but has no difficulty in naming them.

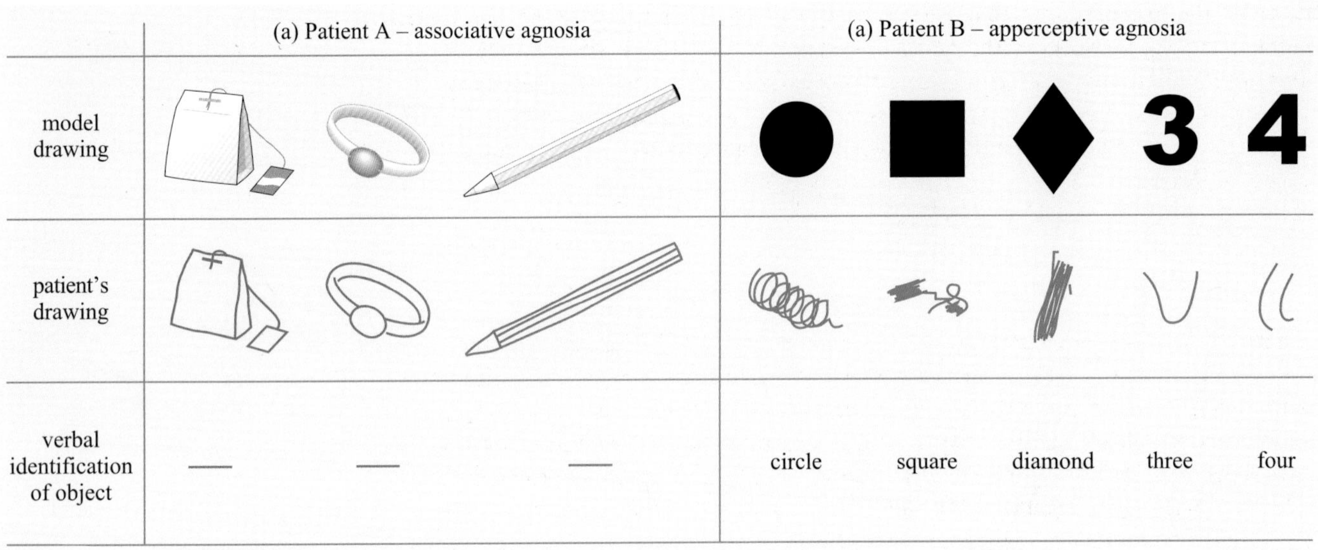

| | (a) Patient A – associative agnosia | | | (a) Patient B – apperceptive agnosia | | | | |
|---|---|---|---|---|---|---|---|---|
| model drawing | | | | ● | ■ | ◆ | 3 | 4 |
| patient's drawing | | | | | | | | |
| verbal identification of object | — | — | — | circle | square | diamond | three | four |

**Figure 1.7**    Selective lesions in the posterior parietal cortex produce selective defects in semantic knowledge. (a) A patient with associative agnosia is able to accurately copy drawings of a teabag, ring, and pencil but is unable to name the objects copied. (b) A patient with apperceptive agnosia is unable to reproduce even simple drawings but nevertheless can name the objects in the drawings.

Further investigation of patients, such as those with associative and apperceptive agnosia, has revealed that episodic and semantic memory does not involve a single, all-purpose memory store, but utilizes the ability of the brain to form multiple representations, each corresponding to a different meaning and capable of being accessed independently. For example when thinking of a particular rose in your garden, you are likely to recall its colour, fragrance, shape, location and texture. Each element is a different representation of a 'rose'; and each can be assessed separately or together – in other words, several cortical regions participate in the generation of the memory, contributing information according to their processing or modal specialization (e.g. smell, vision, taste, touch, emotional context, time).

Memory formation involves at least three distinct processes and some of these were mentioned earlier in Section 1.1.1. The first of these is *encoding* and refers to the ways in which newly learned information is attended to and processed when first encountered. The likelihood of new information entering long-term storage is determined by how well it is attended, associating it meaningfully and systematically with knowledge that is already well established in memory so that it becomes integrated with prior information. The process of encoding is strengthened when the individual is highly motivated, particularly if the information has a strong emotional content. (This will be revisited in the final book of this course.)

*Consolidation* is the second process involved in the formation of new memories, and it refers to those processes that alter the newly stored and still fragile information so as to make it more stable. As you will learn later in this chapter (Section 1.9), consolidation involves a host of biochemical changes that alter the physical properties of the connections made between neurons. Once stored, memories require a retrieval mechanism – a means by which memories can be accessed and appropriately presented.

*Retrieval* is the process that allows us to recall and use stored information. Current knowledge of the retrieval systems employed by the brain is very rudimentary. As mentioned earlier, it is possible that many forms of memory dysfunction might not be due to the loss of storage capacity (i.e. hippocampal or cortical tissue) but instead might reflect some aspect of the retrieval system. Retrieval involves bringing different kinds of information together, representations that are stored separately in different storage sites. Retrieval of memory is much like perception; it is a constructive process and therefore subject to distortion, much as perception is subject to illusions.

### 1.5.2  Spatial learning in mammals and birds: procedural or declarative memory?

The hippocampus plays a central role in spatial memory. (The location and the anatomical divisions of the human hippocampus are shown in Figure 1.8.) It allows us to rapidly form spatial cognitive maps of our surroundings. The evolutionary advantages of this are readily obvious. Such a map, an internal representation of our surroundings, allowed our ancestors to rapidly locate the best escape route or hideaway when threatened with danger or to find the best sources of food and shelter. We all use spatial maps in our everyday existence – navigating busy town centres or locating the fuse box when the lights have failed in a power cut. With the advent of modern non-invasive brain imaging techniques, as described in Book 3, Chapter 2, it is now possible to compare the size of particular brain regions between human individuals. Interestingly, there is a positive correlation between the size of the human hippocampus and the ability to perform complex spatial tasks; this is beautifully illustrated by the London taxi driver study mentioned in Book 1, Section 3.6. It was discovered that London taxi drivers, who by the nature of their employment must possess an extensive knowledge of the street map of London, have a larger posterior hippocampus than non-taxi drivers. Of course, this then poses the question: Are individuals with large hippocampal structures more likely to become taxi drivers or is it the act of acquiring large amounts of spatial information (the street maps) that induces a larger hippocampus?

An answer to this question can be found by studying the brains of food-storing (caching) birds, such as that of the scrub jay (from North America) shown in Figure 1.9.

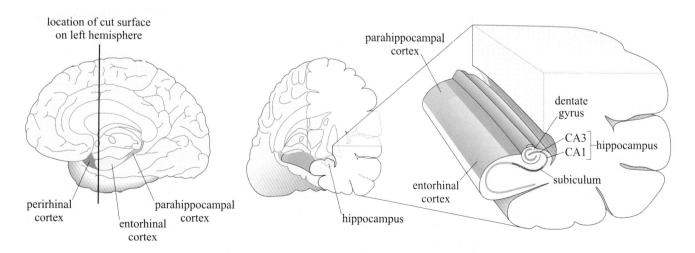

**Figure 1.8**   The human hippocampus revealed. (*left*) A sagittal section of the human brain (also note the location of the perirhinal cortex – we return to the perirhinal cortex in Section 1.8.2). (*middle*) A section taken at the level indicated in the sagittal section on the left. (*right*) An expanded view of the hippocampus. CA1 and CA3 are regions of the hippocampus – these are discussed further in Section 1.7.

**Figure 1.9**   An American western scrub jay (*Aphelocoma californica*) looking for a cache of food hidden in an ice-cube tray.

Scrub jays have remarkable memories for hidden food. In a season, a single bird may store up to 33 000 items of food in as many as 7000 different locations and be able to retrieve them months later, even when the cached food is several feet under snow. This ability seems to reside in the hippocampus of these birds. Avian species that store food have a bigger hippocampus than have closely related species that do not cache food. Food-storing birds are not born with a larger hippocampus, it develops with the experience of hiding and retrieving food caches. It has been shown experimentally that they possess the 'potential' for an enlarged hippocampus. This potential can be lost when the birds are denied any experience of storing and retrieving food and thus do not develop an enlarged hippocampus. A case of 'use it or lose it'.

From a theoretical point of view it should be possible to construct a spatial map using either procedural or declarative means. For example, let us consider how we would direct someone to the local train station. We could say 'To get to the railway station turn left, straight at the traffic lights and then turn right' or we could say 'The railway station is 2 miles south-east of the market square'. The former is an example of a procedural rule, a set of instructions to tell us 'how' to get to the station while the latter is a declarative representation, telling us 'where' the station can be found.

In rodents, the hippocampus is also critical for spatial learning. We know this because rats and mice that have had their hippocampus removed fail to solve or learn a spatial task, but importantly, they still perform well in procedural learning tasks (i.e. the pattern of cognitive sparing and loss is very similar to that of H.M.). One of the most widely used tests for assessing spatial memory in rats and mice is the Morris water maze (Figure 1.10) (Morris, 1984). Briefly, as illustrated in Figure 1.10a, a rat is placed in a circular tank of water containing a submerged platform. The rat cannot see the platform as the water is made opaque by the addition of a little milk, however, the rat can see several visual images or cues that are placed about the maze on the walls of the laboratory. The first time the rat is placed in the water it swims randomly about the tank and when by chance it finds the submerged platform, it will climb onto it to escape the water and to rest (Figure 1.10a). On subsequent testing the rat will learn the location of the platform and will swim to it, using the shortest route (Figure 1.10b). Another way of assessing how well an animal has learnt the location of the hidden platform, is to remove the platform and plot how much time the animal spends swimming in the region where the platform has previously been located. Figure 1.10c shows an example of such a test. (This test is often called the quadrant or probe test.)

Of course the problem here is that the experimenter cannot ask the rat which learning strategy it used to solve the maze. The animal will use visual cues to navigate the maze. This is known because if the visual cues are removed, or repositioned, the animal is no longer capable of finding the platform unless it swims onto it by chance – how it uses the cues in terms of procedural or declarative solutions to locate the platform is less tangible.

Richard Morris, the scientist who developed this water maze, solved this problem by placing the rat in a different location at the beginning of each training session

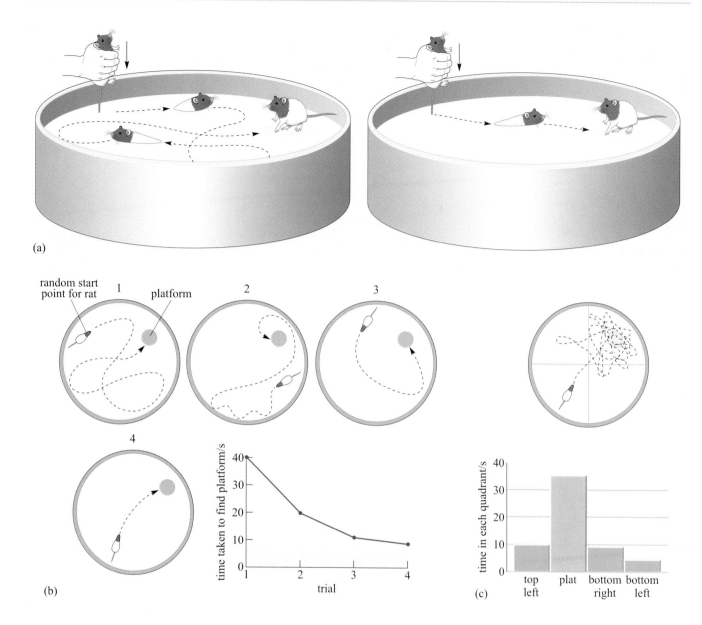

**Figure 1.10** (a) When an animal is first introduced to the Morris water maze, as shown on the left, it swims randomly in the water until it collides, by chance, with the submerged platform, at which point the normal response is to climb onto it. Once an animal has learnt the location of the platform, it swims directly to it, as illustrated on the right. (b) Each time an animal is tested in the water maze, its performance improves. The swim path taken by an animal, over four consecutive trials, is shown. The time taken to find the platform is also plotted. (c) After training, a quadrant test is performed. Note that the animal spends more time in the region (quadrant) where the platform had previously been located.

(also called a trial). The entry point was chosen randomly so that the rat did not know beforehand at which point it would enter the water. In order for the rat to find the platform it first had to orientate itself using the visual cues. This need for orientation, in order to find the platform, indicates the declarative nature of this form of learning. If the rat relied on a procedural solution, it would not be able to find the platform.

◆ Can procedural memory be used to locate the submerged platform in the water maze?

◆ Procedural memory requires the learning of a set of rules to solve a problem or to perform a motor action. In the case of the water maze, the rat would locate the platform by swimming in a pattern according to a set of learnt rules, for example, 'swim to the centre of the tank, then turn right'.

However, because the rat is placed into the water at a random location it is not possible to formulate a solution based on procedural rules. Instead, the animal uses the visual cues to form a spatial cognitive map of the tank, including the precise location of the submerged platform. Irrespective of where the animal enters the water, it is able to locate the platform using this spatial map.

We also use spatial maps, even though when helping others to find a particular location it is often easier to give a set of procedural instructions. The reason for this is that a declarative instruction, such as 'next to the post office', will be of little use if the recipient does not already have a spatial map of the area in question.

### 1.5.3   The failing brain: Alzheimer's disease

Alzheimer's disease (named after Alois Alzheimer, a German psychiatrist who published the first clinical report of this condition in 1901) is the most common form of human dementia (impaired intellectual and cognitive function), accounting for 60–80% of cases in the elderly. It affects about 10% of the population aged over 65, and as many as 45% of people over 85. The earliest sign is typically an impairment of recent declarative memory and attention, followed by progressive deterioration of language skills, visual–spatial orientation, abstract thinking and judgement. Inevitably, severe alteration of personality and a loss of the ability to live independently accompany the terminal stages of this disease.

Diagnosis of Alzheimer's disease, based on the characteristic clinical symptoms just described, is at best tentative and can only be confirmed by postmortem examination of the brain. The pathology of an Alzheimer's diseased brain consists of three principal features. The first is the evident loss of brain volume (i.e. loss of neurons), particularly in the hippocampus, medial lobe and neocortex, as illustrated in Figure 1.11. The second is the presence of large numbers of extracellular deposits (Figure 1.12a), consisting of an abnormal protein called beta-amyloid. These deposits are often referred to as amyloid plaques or senile plaques (Book 1, Figure 2.23). The third feature is also an abnormal aggregation of protein, though in this case the deposits are intracellular. The protein here, called *tau*, forms tangles within the cell that are referred to as *neurofibrillary tangles* (Figure 1.12b). Both the amyloid plaques and the tangles are toxic. As they accumulate in the brain they disrupt the normal functioning of the neurons, eventually killing them.

Brain imaging techniques such as those discussed in Book 3, Chapter 2 now make it possible to measure the volume of the medial lobe or, more specifically, that part of it that comprises the hippocampus in living patients. These studies have revealed a correlation between the severity of the Alzheimer's disease and the loss of brain volume.

◇ Why should medial temporal lobe or hippocampal atrophy be so significant in terms of memory loss?

◆ If you recall, when H.M. had his medial temporal lobe (including the hippocampus) surgically removed to cure his epilepsy, his ability to form new memories was subsequently severely affected.

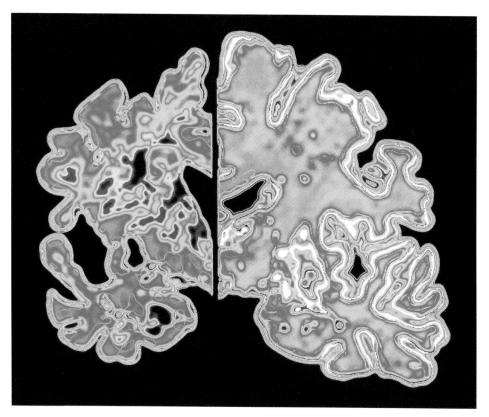

**Figure 1.11** Computer graphic of a coronal section through the brain of a living Alzheimer's patient (*left*) compared with a normal brain (*right*). Note the shrunken state of the diseased brain.

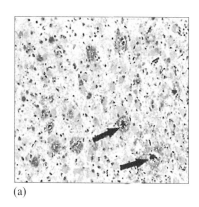

(a)

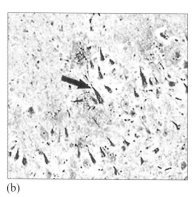

(b)

**Figure 1.12** (a) Extracellular amyloid plaques and (b) intracellular neurofibrillary tangle in Alzheimer's disease. The major constituent of the plaques is beta-amyloid, a toxic peptide liberated from amyloid precursor protein. Tangles contain hyperphosphorylated tau protein. Aggregates are indicated by black arrows.

The vast majority of Alzheimer's disease cases are sporadic and associated with old age. However, a small fraction of cases (less than 1%) is due to a genetic disorder. Identification of the mutant gene in a few affected families with an aggressive and early-onset form of the disease has provided considerable insight into the kinds of processes that can go awry. It appears that a number of mutations can occur in the gene that codes for a protein called the amyloid precursor protein (APP), or in those genes that encode enzymes that are involved in the processing of APP. In Alzheimer's disease, APP is inappropriately cleaved, producing a toxic form of amyloid called beta-amyloid which is released into the extracellular space where it aggregates to form amyloid plaques (Figures 1.12a).

It is possible to assess the involvement or importance of a particular gene mutation in Alzheimer's disease by using molecular genetics to express the mutant gene in mice (Book 3, Section 2.5) – to see if the mice develop the hallmarks of this human disease: memory impairment and the formation of amyloid plaques. Figure 1.13a shows the hippocampus of a mouse that has been genetically altered so that its cells express a mutant form of APP that has been identified in a Swedish family vulnerable to early-onset Alzheimer's disease. The hippocampi of these mice which express the Swedish mutation, clearly show the deposition of amyloid plaques in the extracellular space (Figure 1.13a). Importantly, these mice also show the early alteration in the processing of the tau protein that precedes the formation of neurofibrillary tangles. The alteration involves an increase in the number of phosphate groups attached to the tau protein (hyperphosphorylation). This finding strongly suggests that altered APP processing contributes to both plaque and tangle formation. When tested by a spatial cognitive task, these mice also failed to perform as well as normal animals (see Figure 1.13b). Both the formation of plaques and the impairment of memory function in these mice were dependent on the age of the animals tested, a feature entirely consistent with the human disease condition.

**Figure 1.13**   The hallmarks of Alzheimer's disease, plaque formation and memory dysfunction, can be recapitulated in mice expressing the Swedish mutation in the gene that codes for APP. (a) The presence of beta-amyloid deposits (stained red) in mouse hippocampus. (Scale bar is 250 μm; DG is the dentate gyrus.) (b) The mice show an age-dependent impairment in a learning task. At 2 months of age they perform normally, but by 10 months the mice are cognitively grossly impaired.

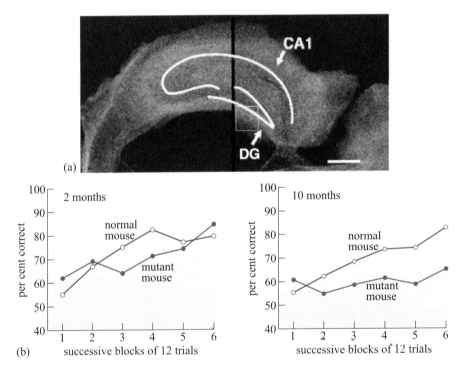

## Summary of Section 1.5

The hippocampus is involved in the acquisition of declarative memory, but is not the long-term store for these memories – instead, memories are slowly transferred to the cerebral cortical storage system.

The case of H.M. exemplifies the assumption that the hippocampus is not involved in procedural learning and memory.

Memory has three distinct phases – encoding, consolidation and retrieval.

# 1.6 The neurobiology of learning and memory

Thus far we have discussed learning and memory in terms of behavioural conditioning and outcomes, with reference to some of the brain regions involved in processing cognitive information. In this section, we will consider the mechanisms used by the brain that allow us to learn and to encode memories.

## 1.6.1 The connectionist view

From the work of Pavlov and others, we have concluded that during learning there is convergence of activity in neural pathways in the brain that brings about a modification of the neural network, possibly in a Hebbian manner, that produces a long-term change in behaviour. So, where is the evidence to support a theory that learning can indeed induce changes in the way that neurons are interconnected?

## 1.6.2 Evidence from 'the deep'

Due to technical limitations it is not yet possible to study changes in individual synapses during learning and memory formation in humans and so this is where the humble sea slug (*Aplysia*, Figure 1.14a) is so important. This small invertebrate has a complex behavioural repertoire, which happens to include a capacity for procedural learning. A remarkable feature of *Aplysia* is that it is possible to record from its neurons whilst the animal is undergoing learning. Furthermore, it is possible to return to the very same neurons days after training to assess the long-term consequences of training on both the neural circuitry and behaviour.

*Aplysia* has approximately 20 000 neurons, and those involved in learning have been identified. It is possible to record electrophysiological responses from a known neuron whilst the animal is learning – allowing a direct correlation to be made between neurobiology and behaviour. By filling a neuron with a dye contained in a recording microelectrode during an experiment, it is possible to examine how its synaptic connections are altered as a consequence of learning. *Aplysia* live in a hostile environment where predation is an ever-present danger so they utilize a wide variety of defensive reflexes to limit or to prevent such harm. These defensive reflex actions include the withdrawal of its external appendages such as its tail, gill and syphon (see Figure 1.14a). For example, tactile stimulation of the sensory neurons located in the syphon will, under normal conditions, cause a defensive reflex withdrawal of the gill. This is because the sensory neurons in the syphon make a direct excitatory synaptic connection with the motor neurons that innervate the muscles responsible for gill withdrawal (Figure 1.14b). Repeated mild stimulation of the syphon will induce a reduction in the gill-withdrawal response – a response know as *habituation* (Figure 1.14c). In contrast to the form of learning displayed by Pavlov's dogs, this form of conditioning is non-associative.

**Figure 1.14**  Modification of a defensive behavioural reflex: habituation in *Aplysia*. (a) A dorsal view of *Aplysia* illustrates the respiratory organ (gill), which is normally covered by the mantle shelf. The mantle shelf ends in the syphon, a fleshy spout used to expel seawater and waste. A tactile (touch) stimulus to the syphon elicits the gill-withdrawal reflex. Repeated stimulation leads to habituation. (b) The sensory and motor neurons are synaptically connected. It is possible to elicit an action potential in the sensory neuron and record the resultant EPSP in the motor neuron. (c) Comparison of the synaptic potentials in a sensory and a motor neuron in a control (untrained) animal and an animal that has been subjected to long-term habituation. In the habituated animal no synaptic potential is evident in the motor neuron one week after training. (d) The reduction in the motor neuron response is due to a decrease in the number of synaptic connections made by the sensory neurons onto the motor neurons. Note that over time the effect of habituation wears off and the number of synapse connections eventually return to the control state.

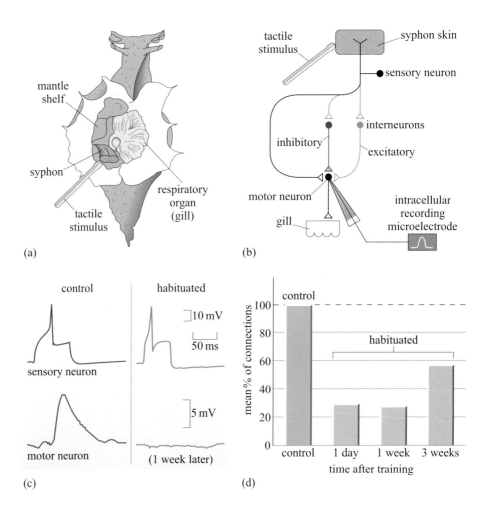

◆  Why is habituation non-associative?

◆  The animal is only exposed to a single type of stimulus and is not required to associate a neutral stimulus with an unconditional response. In the case of habituation, the stimulus becomes less efficient as a means of eliciting their defensive behavioural response, i.e. the stimulus is eventually not regarded as a noxious input.

It is possible to make simultaneous recordings from both the sensory neuron of the syphon and the motor neuron of the gill in *Aplysia*. By using a recording electrode to depolarize the inside of the sensory neuron, it is possible to make the sensory neuron fire an action potential (Book 4, Chapter 1). The resultant EPSP generated in the motor neuron by the neurotransmitter released from the sensory neuron can then be recorded. Experiments like this have shown that the decrease in the gill-withdrawal response is directly attributable to a decrease in the size of the EPSP – in other words, habituation is caused by a decrease in efficiency at the synapse between the sensory and motor neurons. In contrast, *sensitization* of the syphon–gill-withdrawal reflex can be brought about by a single, but intense stimulus applied to the tail or head. A subsequent mild tactile stimulus applied to the syphon then produces a more powerful withdrawal of the gill. Analysis of the EPSP generated in the motor neuron now shows that there has been an increase in the synaptic efficiency between the sensory and motor neurons (see Figure 1.14d).

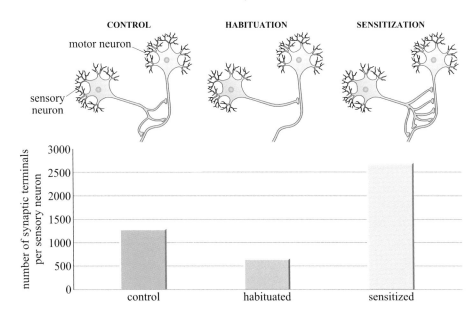

**Figure 1.15** Changes in synaptic connectivity related to learning in *Aplysia*. When measured 1 week after training, the number of presynaptic terminals is highest in the sensitized animals and lowest in the habituated animals, compared to controls.

It is possible to induce forms of habituation and sensitization that last for several days in *Aplysia*. Analysis of the number of synaptic connections made by sensory neurons reveals that habituation is associated with a decrease in the number of synaptic terminals, whereas the converse is true for sensitized animals (Figure 1.15).

◈ What is the relationship between the size of the EPSP recorded in the motor neuron and the number of sensory synaptic connections?

◆ The greater the number of synaptic connections, the larger the size of the EPSP. The converse is also true.

Whilst such overt changes related to single learning events have yet to be demonstrated in the adult mammalian brain, there is nonetheless considerable evidence to suggest that mammalian synapses also undergo conspicuous changes in their ability to process information.

## Summary of Section 1.6

The connectionist view of learning and memory is that information in the brain is encoded by changes in the efficiency of synaptic transmission. It is believed that these changes occur at those synapses involved in the creation and storage of the particular memory.

Simple learning in *Aplysia* is accompanied by changes in the number of synaptic connections between the sensory and motor neurons. Here, an increase in synaptic efficiency is brought about by an increase in the number of synapses, whereas a decrease in efficiency is associated with a loss of synaptic connections.

## 1.7   Hebbian synapses revealed: the hippocampus

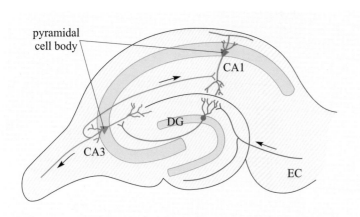

**Figure 1.16**   The hippocampal circuit. The three main regions of the hippocampal formation are shown: CA1, CA3 and the dendate gyrus (DG). The neuronal cell bodies of the CA and DG regions form well-defined layers that can be seen by the naked eye. These neurons are synaptically connected – forming a trisynaptic circuit. The neurons of the DG receive an afferent input from the entorhinal cortex (EC). The DG neurons, in turn, project to the CA3 neurons, and these in turn send a synaptic projection to the CA1 neurons.

Given the importance of the hippocampus for memory, it is not at all surprising to learn that this was one of the first mammalian brain regions to be studied by neurobiologists in the 'hunt' for Hebbian synapses. Fortuitously, the hippocampus lends itself well to electrophysiological investigation. Its neuronal and synaptic circuitry is well organized and is relatively simple (Figure 1.16). The latter is pertinent because it means that recording and stimulating electrodes can be placed within known populations of cells and known afferent pathways. Lastly, it is possible to maintain the hippocampus in tissue culture, preserving the integrity of its neural circuitry. This allows the use of sophisticated electrophysiological techniques and critically, the application of pharmacological agents to investigate and manipulate synaptic function.

Learning is a rapid process, occurring within milliseconds, but its *outcome*, memory, can last for considerable periods of time. Any model for learning must therefore include rapid *induction*, an enduring outcome and be specific to the neural circuitry involved. Most psychologists agree that learning is an activity-driven process. We do not know the precise pattern of activity that occurs at mammalian synapses during learning. It is likely that, for a time, there is an increase in the activity of those synapses involved in encoding the learnt information and that this period of increased activity leads to a change in the strength of the neural network. In the laboratory, it is possible to bring about robust and lasting increases in the efficiency of hippocampal synapses by brief periods of strong activation – a form of activity-dependent synaptic enhancement called **long-term potentiation (LTP)** that was first described by Bliss and Lømo (1973). Figure 1.17 shows an example of LTP recorded in a rat hippocampus that was maintained in tissue culture. A stimulating electrode is used to activate an afferent pathway that makes synaptic connections with a population of hippocampal pyramidal neurons. In the example shown, an extracellular recording electrode is used to record an EPSP in a population of postsynaptic neurons. The afferent pathway is stimulated to evoke an EPSP once every 30 seconds. When the evoked response is stable and does not fluctuate over time, the afferent pathway is then stimulated briefly at a high frequency. (This is called the *conditioning tetanus* and typically consists of a hundred shocks applied at 100 Hz.) This form of conditioning is designed to recreate the conditions that might occur at a Hebbian synapse during learning. By powerfully stimulating the afferent pathway, both the presynaptic and postsynaptic neurons are strongly activated at the same time. Immediately after conditioning, the afferent pathway is then again stimulated once every 30 seconds as before. Note here that the term conditioning refers to the pattern of stimulation applied to the neurons and is not to be confused with the behavioural paradigms used in behavioural experiments.

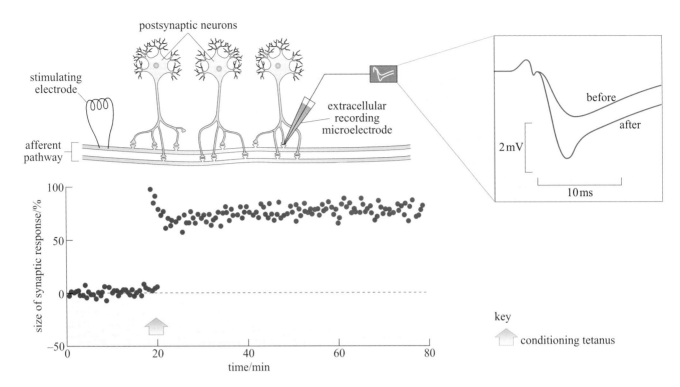

**Figure 1.17** Hippocampal synaptic plasticity – long-term potentiation (LTP). A stimulating electrode is used to stimulate a tract of afferent fibres (the afferent pathway) that make synaptic connections with neurons located in the CA1 region of the hippocampus. The afferent pathway is stimulated once every 30 seconds and the size of the evoked EPSP is plotted graphically against time. Once a stable baseline is achieved, a train of high-frequency shocks (the conditioning tetanus: this consists of 100 shocks applied at 100 Hz) was applied to the afferent pathway via the stimulating electrode. The inset shows the evoked EPSP before and 1 hour after conditioning.

◈ Look at Figure 1.17. What effect does conditioning have on subsequent synaptic transmission?

◆ The responses recorded after the conditioning tetanus are larger than those recorded prior to conditioning – they are said to have become potentiated.

Similar experiments to that shown in Figure 1.17, using electrodes implanted into the hippocampus of living rats and rabbits, have revealed that such changes can last for many days and in some cases for several weeks. It is the lasting nature of this enhancement, induced by a brief but intense period of Hebbian activation, which makes LTP such a compelling neural correlate for learning and memory.

The experiment shown in Figure 1.17 is relatively simple and perhaps at first glance does not directly relate to Pavlov and his dogs. However, as we will discuss later, the molecular and biochemical events that occur at the synapses during conditioning do indeed involve a form of classical conditioning.

Figure 1.18 illustrates some of the key qualities of LTP that make it such a compelling model for learning and memory, and furthermore, it demonstrates all the properties required for classical conditioning. In this experiment, instead of stimulating one set of afferent fibres, a second set is also activated, but not at the same time as the first. One pathway (pathway A) receives a *weak* conditioning tetanus that fails to induce LTP. The second (pathway B) receives a *strong* conditioning tetanus that successfully induces LTP. In terms of classical conditioning, and in particular with respect to Pavlov's dogs, we can think of the

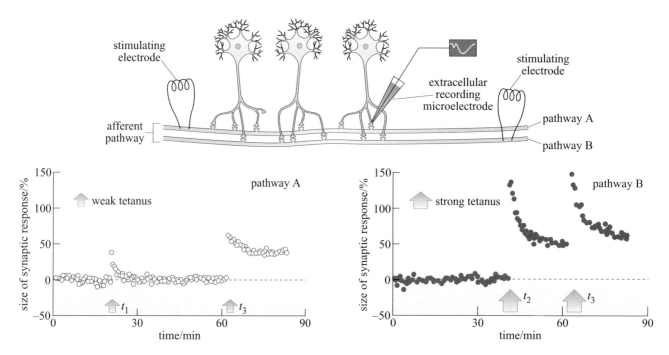

**Figure 1.18**    Associative LTP. A strong tetanus (100 shocks at 100 Hz) applied to pathway B (at $t_2$) induces LTP. Note that the LTP is seen only in pathway B demonstrating the synaptic-specificity of LTP. When a weak tetanus (20 shocks at 50 Hz) is applied to pathway A (at $t_1$) no LTP is induced. When the weak tetanus is applied to pathway A at the same time as the strong tetanus is applied to pathway B (at $t_3$), the weak tetanus is now capable of inducing LTP in pathway A.

weak pathway (pathway A) as representing the auditory input (the bell; the neutral response) and the strong pathway (pathway B) as being the food, and the induction of LTP being the unconditional response (salivation). When the weak tetanus is applied to pathway A in the absence of any other synaptic activity, it fails to induce LTP (the bell alone fails to elicit salivation: $t_1$). Application of the strong tetanus to pathway B successfully induces LTP (the food elicits a salivatory response: $t_2$). However, when the weak tetanus is applied to pathway A at the same time as the strong tetanus is applied to pathway B at $t_3$ (when the bell and food are presented together), LTP is successfully induced in the weak pathway (pathway A), the conditional response. This time, pairing the food with the ringing of the bell has changed synaptic efficiency so that the bell now elicits salivation. This form of LTP is associative – the temporal association of two events, here the co-activation of both pathway A and pathway B, has changed the processing properties of the network.

What does the experiment shown in Figure 1.18 tell us about the properties of LTP? Firstly, it tells us that LTP has a threshold for its induction. For LTP to be successfully induced, an intensity threshold must first be exceeded during the conditioning tetanus – the weak tetanus failed to achieve this but the strong tetanus was successful. This threshold is determined by the level of depolarization achieved in the postsynaptic cells during conditioning; the greater the depolarization, the more likely that LTP will ensue. However, it is not quite that simple because postsynaptic depolarization alone is not sufficient to induce LTP; *it must be paired with the release of neurotransmitter from the presynaptic cell.* In other words, there has to be a conjunction between pre- and postsynaptic activity; this will be explained further in Section 1.8. As a rule, the more afferent fibres that are activated during the tetanus (i.e. cooperate together) the greater the probability that LTP will occur. This property, which is attributable to the number of active afferent fibres that contribute to the depolarization of the postsynaptic cell during conditioning, is called *cooperativity*.

◈ Why is LTP Hebbian?

◆ Because in order to occur, LTP requires co-activation of both the presynaptic and postsynaptic neurons, i.e. the release of neurotransmitter from the presynaptic terminal and while this is happening, depolarization of the postsynaptic neuron.

◈ Why is a threshold for the induction of LTP desirable?

◆ Because without one, synapses might undergo potentiation in a poorly regulated fashion, depleting their value as a means of encoding information.

Another important feature of LTP demonstrated in Figure 1.18, is that LTP is restricted to those synapses that undergo conditioning. The expression of LTP that is induced in pathway B is not transferred to pathway A. Hippocampal neurons (Figure 1.19) can have as many as 10 000 synaptic connections. By limiting the induction of LTP to those synapses that are active during conditioning, the cell dramatically increases its capacity to store information.

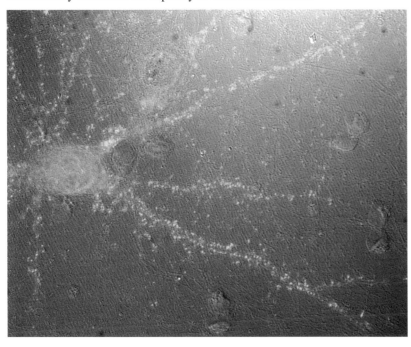

**Figure 1.19**   An image of a living hippocampal cell taken using a fluorescent microscope. The postsynaptic cell has been filled with a red dye. The dendrites of this cell are heavily decorated with small green spots, and each of these is a presynaptic terminal made with the dye-filled neuron.

Alterations in synaptic plasticity, such as LTP, are believed to underlie several brain disorders, including Alzheimer's disease and Huntington's disease.

◈ Look at the data in Figure 1.13b which shows a decline in the learning performance of mice expressing the APP Swedish mutation. What effect do you think this mutation will have on LTP in these animals?

◆ These mice show a clear cognitive deficit at 10 months of age when compared with normal mice. If LTP is positively correlated with learning performance, then these mice should not be able to support LTP by the time they are 10 months old.

Figure 1.20 shows how the expression of the APP Swedish mutation degrades the ability of hippocampal neurons to support LTP. Of course, this in itself is not proof that LTP has anything to do with learning.

**Figure 1.20** Age-dependent impairment of LTP in Swedish APP mice. (a) Mutant mice and normal mice, aged between 2 and 8 months, show similar levels of LTP. (b) Once they are over 15 months of age, the mutant mice fail to sustain LTP.

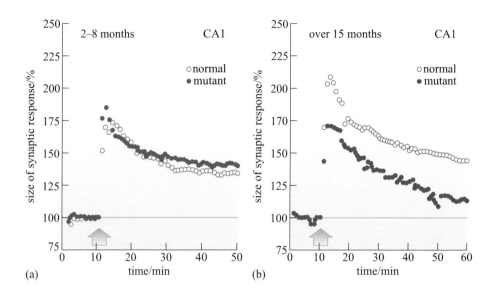

## Summary of Section 1.7

The efficiency of hippocampal synapses can be altered by changes in the pattern of synaptic activity in a manner entirely consistent with the Hebbian synapse first postulated by Donald Hebb. A brief period of high-frequency stimulation applied to an afferent pathway (the conditioning tetanus) can bring about an enduring increase in the size of the postsynaptic potential – a form of synaptic modification called long-term potentiation (LTP). LTP is synapse-specific – only those synapses activated during the conditioning are modified. It is also associative.

# 1.8 The mechanics of a Hebbian synapse

The properties of LTP, particularly at those synapses located in the hippocampus, are largely determined by a postsynaptic glutamate receptor called the *N*-methyl-D-aspartate receptor (NMDA receptor – you were introduced to this receptor in Book 4, Box 1.1). Hippocampal synapses use glutamate as their neurotransmitter. There are two types of glutamate-gated ion channels in the postsynaptic membrane: NMDA receptors and AMPA receptors (Figure 1.21). NMDA receptors are unusual, as unlike other types of glutamate receptors, they are voltage-dependent, a property conferred upon them by extracellular magnesium ions. Hippocampal neurons have resting membrane potentials of about −67 mV to −80 mV. At these relatively negative potentials, positively charged magnesium ions are attracted to the extracellular surface of the plasma membrane of the postsynaptic neuron and some lodge within the NMDA receptor channel pore, effectively blocking the channel (Figure 1.21).

Under normal conditions, the EPSP is mediated almost entirely by AMPA receptors. This is because the NMDA receptor channels are blocked by magnesium ions. However, during the induction of LTP, the increase in presynaptic activity releases sufficient glutamate to depolarize the postsynaptic membrane to a level that repels the magnesium ions from the NMDA channels, allowing ions (in the form of sodium and calcium ions) to pass through them. So, in order for the NMDA channel to open, and thus trigger the induction of LTP, it is necessary for two events to occur simultaneously: the membrane must be depolarized to displace magnesium ions and the neurotransmitter, glutamate, must be bound to its receptor

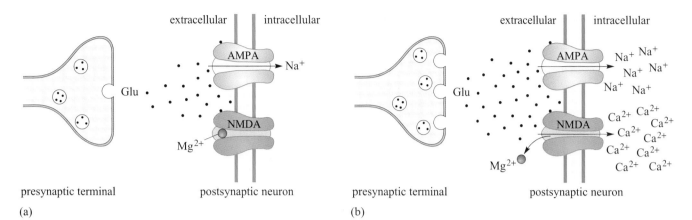

extracellular | intracellular

AMPA → Na+

Glu

NMDA

Mg²⁺

presynaptic terminal          postsynaptic neuron

(a)

extracellular | intracellular

AMPA → Na⁺ Na⁺ Na⁺ Na⁺ Na⁺ Na⁺

Glu

NMDA → Ca²⁺ Ca²⁺ Ca²⁺ Ca²⁺ Ca²⁺ Ca²⁺ Ca²⁺ Ca²⁺ Ca²⁺ Ca²⁺

Mg²⁺

presynaptic terminal          postsynaptic neuron

(b)

site on the NMDA receptor. In other words, the NMDA channel acts as a coincidence detector – it opens only when there is a conjunction of neurotransmitter in the synaptic cleft and a critical level of depolarization in the postsynaptic neuron, a temporal pairing of presynaptic and postsynaptic activation: a Hebbian synapse.

### 1.8.1 The trigger and the maintenance of LTP

As well as being voltage-dependent, NMDA receptors are also permeable to calcium ions. (AMPA receptors are usually impermeable to calcium.) The calcium permeability of the NMDA receptor is a crucial element in the induction of LTP. It is the influx of calcium ions into the postsynaptic cell, via the NMDA channel, that triggers the biochemical cascade that leads to the increase in synaptic efficiency – LTP. Manipulations that reduce the entry or lower the intracellular concentration of calcium all prevent the induction of LTP.

Once induced, LTP persists for hours, even weeks. How is this achieved? First we must consider how a synaptic response might be enhanced. One possibility is that after the induction of LTP, more neurotransmitter is released from the presynaptic terminal upon stimulation. Another is that the postsynaptic membrane and/or its receptors becomes more sensitive, producing a larger level of depolarization upon activation. In other words, LTP could be maintained by either presynaptic or postsynaptic mechanisms.

◆ How might the properties of the postsynaptic membrane be altered so that a larger EPSP is produced after the induction of LTP?

◆ Under normal conditions, the AMPA receptor is the main receptor involved in the generation of the EPSP prior to and after the induction of LTP. (This is because the NMDA receptor channel is blocked by extracellular magnesium, see Figure 1.21a). An increase in the size of the EPSP after the induction of LTP might involve either a change in the properties of the AMPA receptors (so each AMPA channel now produces more depolarization) and/or an increase in the number of functional AMPA receptors. Of course, another possibility is that NMDA receptors lose their sensitivity to extracellular magnesium ions so that they can contribute to the EPSP – however, this is not the case.

**Figure 1.21** The dual role of the NMDA receptor as an activity coincidence detector and gateway for calcium entry during the induction of LTP. (a) During normal low-frequency synaptic transmission (i.e. when the synapses are not involved in learning), the neurotransmitter glutamate (Glu) is released from the presynaptic terminal where it binds to both NMDA and AMPA receptors on the postsynaptic neuron. Because the channel of the NMDA receptor is blocked by extracellular magnesium ions, only the AMPA receptors contribute to the generation of the synaptic potential. (b) During the induction of LTP, more glutamate is released from the presynaptic terminals, generating more depolarization in the postsynaptic cell – this now repels the magnesium ions from the NMDA receptor, allowing calcium ions to enter the neuron. It is the entry of calcium into the postsynaptic neuron that triggers the biochemical cascade that gives rise to LTP.

Changes in the properties and increases in the number of AMPA receptors have been implicated in the maintenance of LTP. The entry of calcium (due to the unblocking of the NMDA receptors) into the postsynaptic neuron during the induction of LTP activates a number of calcium-dependent intracellular enzymes called **kinases**; proteins which regulate the function of other proteins by adding phosphate groups to them. Some of these kinases can directly alter the properties of the AMPA receptor so that more ions can pass through the AMPA receptor channel, whilst other kinases regulate the insertion of new AMPA receptors into the postsynaptic membrane.

Presynaptic involvement in the maintenance of LTP has proved controversial. Whilst there is considerable evidence to support the view that there is an increase in neurotransmitter release after the induction of LTP, the conundrum is, how does the presynaptic terminal know that it has been potentiated? The problem here is that the NMDA receptors involved in the induction of LTP are located on the postsynaptic membrane. Blockade of these receptors with an antagonist prevents the induction of LTP, and therefore the antagonist must also prevent the presynaptic manifestation of LTP: an increase in neurotransmitter release. In some way, activation of NMDA receptors during the induction of LTP must give rise to a signal that activates the presynaptic terminal. As discussed in Book 4, Chapter 1, chemical synapses are uni-directional – information, via the agency of a neurotransmitter, flows from the presynaptic terminal to the postsynaptic membrane. As the postsynaptic cell does not possess the neurotransmitter vesicular release mechanisms found in presynaptic terminals, how can it generate a signal, a retrograde messenger, that is able to pass from the postsynaptic cell to the presynaptic terminal?

It appears that the postsynaptic cell makes use of two biochemical pathways to generate retrograde messengers – pathways that are activated by the entry of calcium through the NMDA receptor. The first pathway results in the release of arachidonic acid into the synaptic cleft. The second pathway involves the generation of the free radical nitric oxide (NO), a gaseous molecule which readily passes through the postsynaptic membrane. Both messengers, once released, then rapidly diffuse to their sites of action at the presynaptic terminal. Arachidonic acid is derived from the plasma membrane itself and NO is a gas that can permeate membranes so the postsynaptic cell does not need to use vesicles as a release mechanism. Retrograde messengers do not act like neurotransmitters, nor are they released in the same large quantities. Instead, they should be thought of as subtle but powerful triggers that facilitate the enhancement of neurotransmitter release from the presynaptic terminal.

The relative importance of post- and presynaptic mechanisms in the maintenance of LTP remains to be fully elucidated, however, it is very likely that synapses employ a mixture of the two.

Whilst LTP does not appear to be associated with overt changes in the number of synaptic connections, such as that seen in *Aplysia*, there is evidence to suggest that the morphology and the number of synapses is altered. Indeed, similar changes have been reported in rats that have undergone intensive training. These studies represent an exciting possibility that in time it might prove possible to trace a living memory in our brains at a synaptic level. However, it should be noted that it is extremely unlikely that a specific memory will be encoded at a single synapse – it is more likely that memories exist in groupings of neurons that are synaptically interconnected.

## 1.8.2  Synaptic depression and learning: knowing what is familiar

Not all forms of learning involve increases in synaptic efficacy, as we have found with habituation in *Aplysia*. In mammals, activity-dependent decreases in synaptic strength are also believed to contribute to cognitive processing. One example is object recognition memory, the process by which we recognize that an object is no longer novel, but is now familiar – a similar process occurs with faces. Recognition memory involves several brain regions including the prefrontal cortex, the hippocampus and a region of the cortex called the perirhinal cortex (see Figure 1.8); damage to the latter, in particular, has a severe and specific effect on recognition memory. Figure 1.22 illustrates how the firing rate of perirhinal cortical neurons encodes the familiarity of an object. Recordings made from individual perirhinal neurons have shown that these cells respond to novel objects by dramatically increasing their firing rate. Over time, on repeated presentations, the object evokes an ever decreasing response and eventually fails to elicit any change in cell firing. In other words, as the object becomes familiar, the perirhinal neurons are less likely to respond. The mechanism underlying the reduction in firing involves a decrease in the efficiency of cortical glutamatergic synapses – a process that instead of producing an enhancement of synaptic transmission as in LTP, now induces a form of enduring depression called long-term depression (LTD). An example of LTD at perirhinal synapses is shown in Figure 1.22.

**Figure 1.22**  Recognition memory. The perirhinal cortex is found on the inferior aspect of the cerebral cortex. (EC is the entorhinal cortex; TE is the temporal cortex.) (a) The firing of a perirhinal cortical neuron is recorded in a monkey. When the monkey is shown a novel image, the cortical neuron responds by increasing its action potential firing rate. (b) As the image becomes familiar after several presentations, the cortical neuron fails to respond – the image in no longer recognized as being 'novel'. (c) Long-term depression (LTD) of synaptic responses recorded in the perirhinal cortex of a mouse. (The bar indicates the conditioning period which consisted of 900 shocks applied to the presynaptic neurons for 15 minutes.)

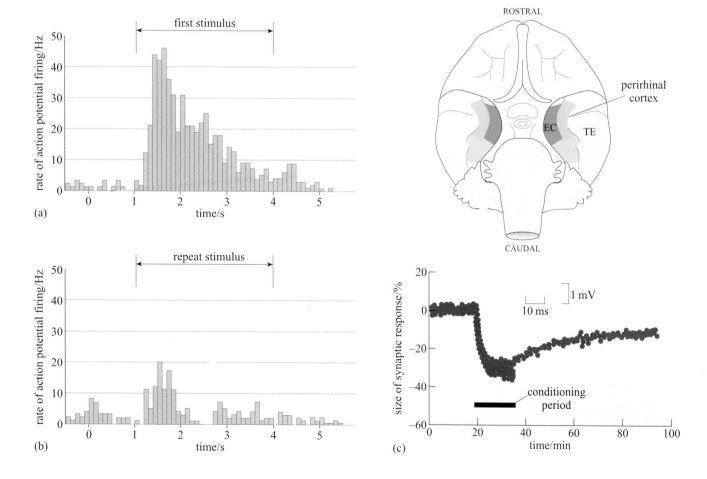

Under experimental conditions, LTD can also be induced in the hippocampus. In contrast to hippocampal LTP, which requires an intense period of synaptic activity, LTD is induced by a prolonged period of low-frequency stimulation. The importance of hippocampal LTD in cognitive processing is currently a matter of intense debate, though it is likely that the role of LTD is to regulate synaptic strength during the development of the hippocampus.

## Summary of Section 1.8

The efficiency of hippocampal synapses can be increased by a brief period of intense activation – pairing strong presynaptic activity with postsynaptic depolarization in a manner which is consistent with a Hebbian learning. This form of synaptic plasticity is called long-term potentiation or LTP.

LTP can be induced at weakly stimulated synapses by pairing activity at these synapses with a stronger stimulus applied to a second set of synapses. By pairing activity in weakly and strongly activated afferent pathways it is possible to modify the efficiency of the weak pathway in a manner that is both Pavlovian and Hebbian.

The Hebbian and Pavlovian properties of LTP are attributable to the NMDA receptor, which acts as a coincidence detector. It is the entry of calcium ions into the postsynaptic neuron via the NMDA receptor that triggers the induction and maintenance of LTP.

# 1.9   Is LTP learning?

## 1.9.1   NMDA receptors and beyond the synapse

Whilst LTP may be a compelling experimental model for the synaptic basis of learning, and demonstrates the properties one would require in a memory device, it remains just that, an experimental model. In the final sections of the chapter we will review recent evidence that develops the link between LTP and learning and memory.

In Section 1.5.2 you were introduced to the Morris water maze and the concept of a spatial map. The formation of spatial memory is critically dependent on the hippocampus and the activation of NMDA receptors. Figure 1.23 shows the swim paths of rats trained in a water maze. One group of animals was given a drug that blocks NMDA receptors and a second group was given saline. The saline-treated animals (Figure 1.23a) were able to learn the location of the hidden platform whereas the animals treated with the NMDA receptor blocker were not (Figure 1.23b). Importantly, when the drug-treated animals were placed in a different water maze, one in which they had been previously successfully trained, they were still capable of finding (remembering) the location of the platform. These observations demonstrate that NMDA receptors are essential for learning but not for memory recall. Given the involvement of NMDA receptors in both spatial learning and the induction of hippocampal LTP, it is very tempting to suggest that the two are one and the same thing. Further evidence comes from mutant mice with NMDA receptors which are functionally silent or impaired. Such mice fail to show LTP or to perform adequately in a spatial learning task.

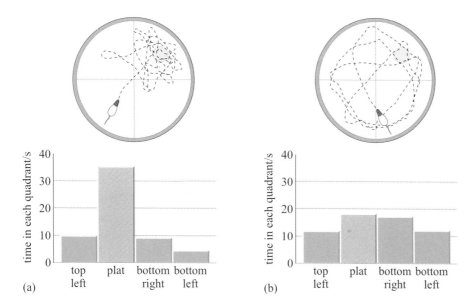

**Figure 1.23** NMDA receptors are required for spatial learning. Rats trained in a water maze were give a quadrant test in which the hidden platform was removed from the tank and the animals allowed to swim for 60 seconds. (a) Control animals (treated with saline) swam persistently in the vicinity of the platform (abbreviated to plat), while (b) those treated with a drug that antagonizes NMDA receptors did not (presumably because they had not learnt the location of the platform).

## 1.9.2 NMDA receptors and new proteins?

At the beginning of this chapter you were introduced to the idea that memories, in terms of their persistence, can be divided into three forms: working memory, short-term memory (STM) and long-term memory (LTM). It appears that the NMDA receptor plays a critical role, not only in the induction of learning, but also in the transition of information from STM to LTM. In the latter case, NMDA receptors can initiate the process of memory *consolidation*.

If you recall from Section 1.1.2, a head injury induces retrograde amnesia, suggesting that in its earliest stages, memory is vulnerable. During this early period, memories remain fragile because their maintenance (or persistence) relies on the cellular and synaptic proteins already present at the synapses and their nearby dendrites. In order for a memory to become permanent (consolidation), there is an *absolute* requirement for the synthesis of new proteins – proteins that will enable the synapse to maintain its enhanced state and therefore sustain the newly encoded information in LTM. Head injuries and electroconvulsive shock therapy interfere with this process, so that memories that were in STM prior to injury or therapy fail to make the transition to LTM.

By using drugs that prevent protein synthesis it is possible to block the consolidation of memory. Figure 1.24 shows the action of the protein synthesis inhibitor cylcoheximide on learning and memory recall. Mice treated with the drug learn the task at the same rate as control mice (treated with saline), however, after training they quickly become amnesic and by 3 hours after training they have no recall of the task at all.

**Figure 1.24** Inhibition of protein synthesis by the drug cycloheximide does not affect learning, but prevents retention of the memory as tested by memory recall. Following inhibition of 90–95% of brain protein synthesis, mice learn at a normal rate, but amnesia develops gradually thereafter.

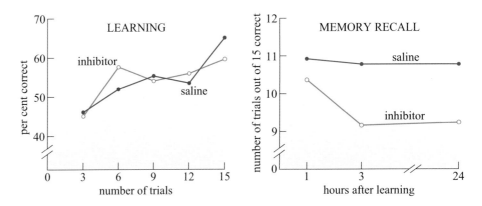

The same drugs that make animals amnesic also affect the expression of LTP, and this pattern of altered expression might provide an explanation for the transient nature of learning seen in drug-treated animals. Under normal conditions, hippocampal LTP lasts for hours, days and even weeks. However, in the presence of a protein synthesis inhibitor, potentiated synaptic responses are maintained for only an hour or so before declining back to pre-conditioning levels – perhaps this is a neural correlate for retrograde amnesia (Figure 1.25). The temporal parallels between slow-onset amnesia and the failure to maintain LTP in these experiments is again compelling evidence that LTP may underlie learning, though of course this still remains a correlation and not proof that LTP encodes learning.

**Figure 1.25** The late-phase maintenance of LTP is prevented by a protein synthesis inhibitor.

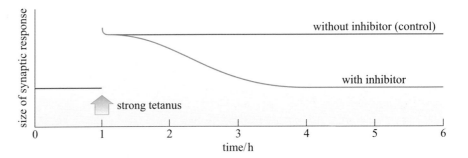

NMDA receptors play a central role in the initiation of protein synthesis: they are believed to activate a local signalling system which identifies newly potentiated synapses for the incorporation of newly synthesized proteins (a process called *synaptic tagging*). The NMDA receptor is not the sole means of activating protein synthesis, but for the purposes of this chapter you do not need to consider these other mechanisms. Activation of NMDA receptors during conditioning or learning induces short-lasting LTP or STM. Strong activation of NMDA receptors also initiates protein synthesis, increasing the likelihood that LTP will be maintained and that the memories in STM will enter LTM.

◆ Can you think of an experiment that will prove or disprove the notion that LTP is the neural correlate for learning?

◆ The most convincing evidence is to show a Pavlovian change in synaptic strength associated with a learning event.

Perhaps the most convincing evidence that information is stored at a synaptic level, using a Hebbian mechanism, comes from the elegant experiments of Le Doux and

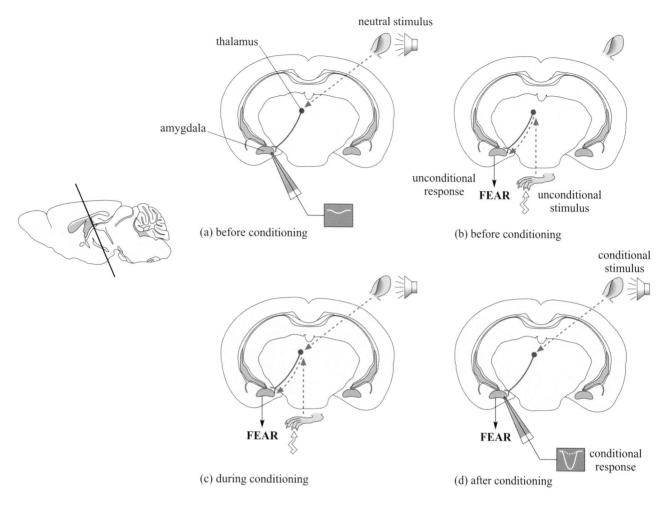

neutral stimulus

thalamus

amygdala

(a) before conditioning

unconditional
response    **FEAR**    unconditional
stimulus

(b) before conditioning

conditional
stimulus

**FEAR**

(c) during conditioning

**FEAR**    conditional
response

(d) after conditioning

colleagues (Rogan *et al.*, 1997). When perturbed or fearful, one of the possible ways in which a rat may respond is to freeze (remain very still). This behavioural response to fear is regulated by the amygdala, a brain structure intimately involved in emotion (Book 6, Chapter 2). In the laboratory a neutral sound such as a tone does not usually evoke freezing in a rat. This is because the rat does not recognize the tone as a fear-inducing stimulus. On the other hand, if the animal receives an electrical shock to its foot, it will respond by freezing. By pairing the presentation of the tone together with a foot shock it is possible to induce a form of classical conditioning such that when the tone is presented alone the animal will freeze. Le Doux used this paradigm to condition a group of rats (Figure 1.26).

Le Doux also used recording electrodes to monitor synaptic responses elicited in the amygdala by the tone. He discovered that after conditioning, the synaptic potentials evoked by the tone were greatly enhanced compared with animals that were exposed to the tone and shock in a random, non-paired manner. Importantly, this enhancement lasted as long as the animals responded to the tone by freezing (Figure 1.27). Further experiments revealed that these synaptic potentials were mediated by glutamatergic receptors and that NMDA receptors were necessary for the synaptic enhancement of the auditory response and for sustained freezing to occur. So, in short, here we have direct and compelling experimental evidence for the involvement of NMDA receptors and synaptic potentiation in a behavioural learning paradigm – the perfect conjunction of psychology with neurobiology!

**Figure 1.26** (*left*) An oblique coronal section shows the position of the amygdala and the thalamus. (a) A tone, activating an auditory input to the thalamus, is used to elicit an EPSP in the amygdala (recorded using an extracellular electrode). The tone when applied alone elicits a small EPSP, but not a fearful response (i.e. freezing), whereas, an electrical shock applied to the foot pad will evoke freezing (b). (c) The animal is then conditioned by repeatedly pairing the presentation of the tone with an electric shock applied to the foot pad. (d) After conditioning, the tone, when applied alone, produces a fearful response – the animal now freezes on hearing the tone. Note that the tone now also produces a larger EPSP – the auditory input to the amygdala is now potentiated.

**Figure 1.27**   A change in mammalian behaviour associated with LTP. The increase in freezing behaviour is correlated with an increase in the size of the amygdalar EPSP. The size of the synaptic potential recorded in the amygdala, and the amount of freezing, are shown for both conditioned and control animals. During the conditioning period, only the conditioned animals received both the tone and the electric shock at the same time. The control animals were exposed to the tone and the shocks, but these were not paired events.

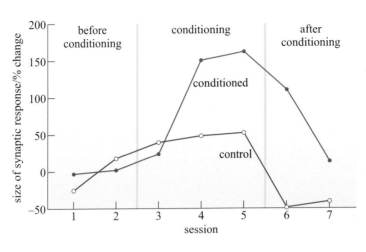

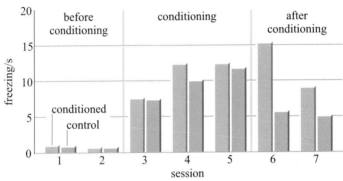

## Summary of Section 1.9

Activation of the NMDA receptor is required for some forms of learning. Both LTP and memory consolidation require the synthesis of new proteins.

## 1.10   Memories that do not involve lasting synaptic modification: working memory revisited

Short-lived memories that do not enter STM or LTM, such as some of those involved in working memory, do not require enduring modification of synaptic connections. Instead, they are maintained by a temporary increase in action potential activity within pre-existing neural networks. The prefrontal cortex is involved in processing working memory, particularly in the timing of the sequence of actions required to perform a working memory-dependent task. In monkeys, damage to the prefrontal cortex impairs a type of non-verbal working memory (visuospatial working memory) that requires the animal to recall a particular location in space. (It is difficult to assess verbal working memory in a monkey as they lack the capacity for complex spoken language.) Prefrontal neurons code for information in the visual field and hold this information by increasing their action potential firing rate; an example is shown in Figure 1.28. Their role is not only to remember particular places within the visual field but also to guide eye movements to those places. This has been demonstrated in the laboratory where eye movements can be used as a precise measure of the animal's working memory. In the experiment shown in Figure 1.28, a monkey was trained to fix its gaze on a circular spot on a screen while it used its peripheral vision to detect a square cue that was flashed briefly at one of eight positions in the visual field. After a delay of several seconds the animal was directed to turn its eyes to where the cue had been. Thus the animal had to keep information about the position of the square cue in working memory for several seconds. In Figure 1.28, the firing rate of a prefrontal neuron is shown. Notice how it increases its firing during the delay period, holding information about the location of the square. If this animal had been distracted during the delay period, say by a loud sound or activity elsewhere in the visual field, the information held in working memory would be lost and seen as a sudden decrease in the firing rate of the neurons involved.

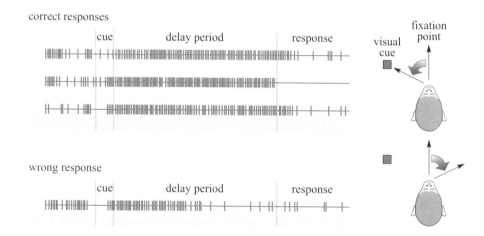

**Figure 1.28** Working memory – neuronal firing as a temporary information store. The records show the firing of a cortical neuron of a monkey during an oculomotor delayed-response task. The animal has been taught to fixate on (or stare at) the centre of a television screen – in other words, fixate at the centre of its visual field. Whilst the animal is fixated, a visual cue is presented on the left-hand side for 0.5 s. The animal is required to continue to stare at the centre of the visual field during a delay period following the presentation of the cue. At the end of the delay period, a signal is given for the animal to turn its eyes to where the cue had been located. On trials in which the monkey correctly turned its eyes to the left (upper traces, on the left), the neuron fired throughout the delay period. On the trial in which the animal was distracted and incorrectly turned its eyes to the right (lower trace), the neuron began to fire but then almost completely stopped firing after 3 s. Some neurons failed to show any increase in firing during the delay when the animal made an incorrect response.

Repeated rehearsal of the information held in working memory can strengthen the memory, eventually facilitating its transfer to STM and LTM. So, how does a piece of information end up in the LTM? Current evidence suggests that, in the first instance, memory starts with some form of sensory event, the raw input. This information, the sensory event, is then recoded to enter working memory. This memory store has a limited capacity (only up to 7 items of information can be held at any one time) and information held in working memory has a tendency to decay over the course of 10 seconds or so, unless it is actively rehearsed. A key feature of working memory is that it only exists in a 'conscious' form, which means that it is highly vulnerable and information stored in working memory can be easily lost if distracted.

### 1.10.1  Forgetting

Some years ago, a poll showed that 84% of psychologists agreed with the statement that 'everything we learn is permanently stored in the mind, although sometimes particular details are not accessible'. The 16% who thought otherwise should get higher marks! There is now growing evidence that forgetting is an important component of memory. Were it not for forgetting, our brains would be impossibly burdened with a welter of useless information. In fact, it appears that the human brain is very good at forgetting. Figure 1.29 shows that the memory of the appearance of an American one cent coin (an icon seen thousands of times by every American since childhood) is uncertain at best. The ability of people to recall television programmes that they have seen several years ago declines with time and this is illustrated in Figure 1.29b.

The capacity to forget unimportant information may be critical for normal comprehension – knowing what to retain being a significant asset. One reason for this presumption is rare individuals who have difficulty in ridding their minds of trivial information. Perhaps the best known case is a subject studied over several decades by the Russian psychologist A. R. Luria, who referred to the subject simply as 'S'. The description of an early encounter below gives some indication of why S, then a newspaper reporter, was so interesting:

> I gave S a series of words, then numbers, then letters, reading them to him slowly or presenting them in written form. He read or listened attentively and then repeated the material exactly as it had been presented. I increased the number of elements in each series, giving him as many as thirty, fifty, or even seventy words or numbers, but this too presented no problem for him. He did not need to commit any of the material to memory; if I gave him a series of words or numbers, which I read slowly and distinctly, he would listen attentively, sometimes ask me to stop and enunciate a word more clearly, or, if in doubt whether he had heard a word correctly, would ask me to repeat it. Usually during an experiment he would close his eyes or stare into space, fixing his gaze on one point; when the experiment was over, he would ask that we pause while he went over the material in his mind to see if he had retained it. Thereupon, without another moment's pause, he would reproduce the series that had been read to him.
>
> A. R. Luria (1987) *The Mind of a Mnemonist*

S's phenomenal memory, however, did not always serve him well. He had difficulty ridding his mind of the trivial information that he tended to focus on, sometimes to the point of incapacitation. As Luria put it:

> Thus, trying to understand a passage, to grasp the information it contains (which other people accomplish by singling out what is most important) became a tortuous procedure for S, a struggle against images that kept rising to the surface in his mind. Images, then, proved an obstacle as well as an aid to learning in that they prevented S from concentrating on what was essential. Moreover, since these images tended to jam together, producing still more images, he was carried so far adrift that he was forced to go back and rethink the entire passage. Consequently, a simple passage – a phrase, for that matter – would turn out to be a Sisyphean task.
>
> A. R. Luria (1987) *The Mind of a Mnemonist*

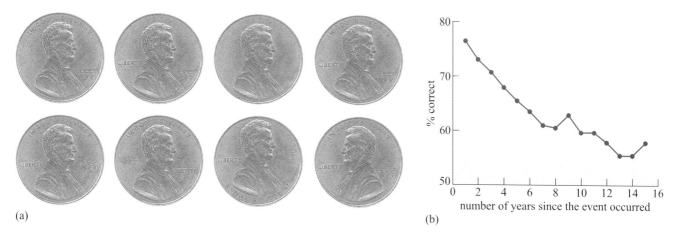

(a)                                                                                                    (b)

**Figure 1.29**   (a) Different version of the 'cent' side of an American one cent coin. Despite innumerable exposures to this familiar design, few Americans are able to pick out the top right cent as the authentic version. Clearly repeated information is not necessarily retained. (b) The deterioration of long-term memories was evaluated in this example by a multiple-choice test in which the subjects were asked to recognize the names of television programmes that had been broadcast for only one season during the past 15 years. Forgetting of stored information that is no longer used evidently occurs gradually and progressively over the years.

So you may console yourself that, when studying with the OU, the fact that you may occasionally have difficulty in recalling information is simply the consequence of normal memory function. Of course, those memories that have a high emotional or arousal content, or were acquired during periods of heightened attention, are the more enduring – perhaps you might want to consider the latter when studying!

◈   How might a neurobiologist explain forgetting?

◆   A neurobiologist would tentatively suggest that forgetting is caused by the decline of LTP at those synapses involved in encoding the failing memory.

## Summary of Section 1.10

It is likely that not all memory is encoded as long-term changes in synaptic efficiency. Some memories, particularly those that only last for a few seconds or less, are believed to exist as a temporary increase in neuronal firing.

## 1.11   Summary of Chapter 1

In conclusion, we want to ensure that you appreciate the wide applicability of all the material considered. At the end of a chapter that has focused on the learning of specific stimuli and behaviours, it is worth recalling that learning is a general process. When any stimuli cause synapses to be activated, it is likely that the synaptic strengths will be modified: some degree of learning of the event will have taken place. Furthermore, although this chapter has given many examples of conditioning in animals, it should be noted that humans too are conditioned. For example, the feedback we receive from others, in response to our behaviour, can have a rewarding or punishing effect, and so increase or decrease the likelihood that we will repeat the behaviour. An example that is often cited is of the naughty child who continues to 'play up', in spite of repeated admonitions. The complaints that the behaviour attracts are considered to be welcomed as attention by the child, and so thought to serve as reinforcers.

For readers who are trying to learn and remember for an examination, a chapter on learning and memory should be able to provide some useful hints. This conclusion to the chapter will focus briefly on some of the themes we have explored, and suggest ways in which you might use the information to aid your study.

### 1.11.1   Depth of processing

You may recall that looking for specific letters in a word list did not help you to remember the list as much as looking for a particular category of word. Letter judgements require only superficial processing, whereas category judgements are an example of deeper analysis. Material is always learned better if it is the subject of extensive processing. If you intend to remember, it is necessary to do far more than just skim-reading the material. Endeavour to process it deeply, thinking about its meaning and implications.

### 1.11.2   Interconnectedness

Recall is more effective when there are strong links between a wide range of related material; this offers a greater chance of one memory triggering another. As you read, try to think of other material with which the current theme may have links; try to find areas of contradiction or support. For example, you will notice that working hard to find connections is a form of deep processing which therefore links with the ideas presented in Sections 1.5, 1.6 and 1.7.

### 1.11.3   Reinforcement and shaping

You do not wish to learn an aversion to your work, like a nauseous rat to saccharine! Try to enjoy the material; don't work for such long periods that it becomes drudgery. Break up your study period and reward yourself at each break; a reward can be as simple as a cup of tea or getting up to look out of the window for a few moments.

### 1.11.4   Strengthening synapses

Synapses grow stronger with repetition. Do not try to commit material to memory then retrieve it just once. Each time you take one of your frequent breaks, spend a short time thinking back over what you have read and try to remember all the significant points. If some seem to be missing, go back and remind yourself.

## Learning outcomes for Chapter 1

At the end of this chapter you should be able to:

1.1 Recognize definitions and applications of each of the terms printed in **bold** in the text.

1.2 Demonstrate knowledge of the classification system used to define different forms of learning and memory.

1.3 Understand the differences between declarative and procedural memory.

1.4 Describe a Hebbian synapse.

1.5 Evaluate the role of the hippocampus in the acquisition of memory.

1.6 Demonstrate an understanding of the synaptic basis of memory.

1.7 Discuss the relevance of LTP with respect to learning and memory.

# Questions for Chapter 1

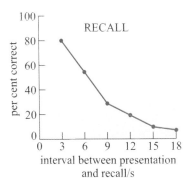

**Figure 1.30**  For use with Question 1.1.

## Question 1.1   *(Learning outcome 1.2)*

For the moment, think of yourself as a willing participant in a psychology experiment. You are presented with three consonants (for example CHJ), forming what is known as a nonsense syllable and, following an interval, you are asked to recall them. The length of the interval varies from trial to trial. You notice that when you are allowed to rehearse the syllable your recall is much improved, however, when you are not allowed to do so, your recall is poor. The outcome of your test is shown in Figure 1.30. What type of memory is being assessed and how could rehearsal improve your score?

## Question 1.2   *(Learning outcomes 1.3 and 1.5)*

In mammals with damage to the hippocampus, certain simple motor skills can be learnt, but more complex learning such as that normally shown in the Morris water maze cannot occur. Why should this be so?

## Question 1.3   *(Learning outcomes 1.3 and 1.5)*

A brain-damaged woman in North America showed the following characteristics: she could remember her name, early childhood, the assassination of President Kennedy, etc. and could conduct a normal conversation. However, although her doctor met her every day, she showed few signs of recognizing the doctor or remembering anything from the previous day's consultation. In terms of consolidation and retrieval of memory, in what way was she abnormal?

## Question 1.4   *(Learning outcomes 1.2 and 1.6)*

After injection of substances that inhibit protein synthesis, which of the following might be expected?

A   Neuron activity would be hindered because of increased ion permeability.

B   Memory formation would be prevented because protein synthesis inhibitors cause excessively increased neurotransmission across the synapse.

C   Neuronal firing would be increased, making consolidation easier.

D   The formation of the morphological/synaptic changes in the nervous system that constitute long-term memory would be hindered or prevented.

E   Short-term memory would be obliterated.

F   The transfer of each short-term memory to its corresponding specific stable molecule code would be prevented.

## Question 1.5   *(Learning outcomes 1.4, 1.6 and 1.7)*

Which of the following statements are true and which are false?

A   A Hebbian synapse is one which is potentiated when neurotransmitter is released from its presynaptic terminal.

B   The NMDA receptor is involved in the induction of LTP but not learning.

C   The NMDA receptor is unusual because, unlike most other neurotransmitter-gated receptors, it is voltage-dependent.

D   The voltage-dependency of the NMDA receptor gives it its Hebbian characteristics.

E   The NMDA receptor is permeable to magnesium ions and is blocked by calcium ions.

F   LTP is the only form of lasting synaptic modification in the mammalian brain.

# FROM SOUND TO MEANING: HEARING, SPEECH AND LANGUAGE

## 2.1 Introduction

As you walk down the street one day, you hear a voice from somewhere behind you that seems to be discussing this course. It says:

> 'My dad's tutor's no joker, and he told me the TMA's going to hit home with a bang.'

You turn to find the face behind the voice, which is a gravelly Glaswegian baritone, but the man has gone, leaving you to ponder what he has said. Let us call his sentence example (1). We will come back to it throughout the chapter.

At the same moment, in Amboseli National Park in Kenya, a group of vervet monkeys (Figure 2.1) is foraging on the ground near a large baobab tree. A young male on the periphery of the group suddenly stands on his hind legs, and gives a loud triple barking sound. The other monkeys have no doubt what this means; a snake is in the vicinity. The monkeys group together, scouring the grass for the location of the predator.

In both these scenarios, a primate brain performed one of its most remarkable tricks. It took a pattern of vibration off the air, and turned it into a very specific set of meanings. How the brain achieves this trick is the subject of this chapter. The monkey example is interesting because it has been seen as a model of the early stages of human language. Vervet monkeys have several distinct alarm calls – *snake*, *leopard* and *eagle* are the best

**Figure 2.1**   Vervet monkeys (*Cercopithecus aethiops*).

studied – each one of which can be said very definitely to have a meaning. We know this because on hearing an eagle call played back by a researcher's tape recorder, the monkeys scan the skies, whilst when a leopard call is played, they climb a tree (Seyfarth *et al.*, 1980). Thus quite different associations are being evoked in the vervet brain.

But in this chapter, the vervet monkey example will mainly be used as an illustration of how different human language is from the communication system of any other primate. The computational task for the human brain in understanding a single sentence is vastly more complex than the vervet case, at every level. It is so complex that a whole field of research – linguistics – is devoted to investigating what goes on, and it requires a whole set of brain machinery that we are only beginning to identify. Hearing and understanding a sentence, or the reverse, where a thought in the brain is turned into a string of buzzes, clicks and notes we call speech, is the crowning achievement of human evolution and the defining feature of human mental life. No other species that we know about comes even close, as the examples below will illustrate.

---

**Activity 2.1**

Write down the main ways in which you think that human language and the call system of the vervet monkey might differ. Keep this list with you and compare it with the differences mentioned in the text as you go through the first half of this chapter.

---

This chapter is in two parts. In the first half (Section 2.2), we will investigate the nature and structure of human language, keeping our vervet monkey example on hand at all times as a comparison. The aim of this first half is to come to a precise understanding of just what the task is that the brain has to perform in processing language. This paves the way for the second half of the chapter (Section 2.3), where we consider different lines of evidence on how and where in the brain this feat is achieved.

## 2.2    The brain's task: the structure of language

### 2.2.1    Preliminaries

To talk about how human language works, we need to establish the meaning of some key terms. The study of language and languages is called linguistics, and linguistics relates closely to biological psychology, as we shall see. Linguists talk about the **grammar** of a language. By this they don't mean a set of rules about how people should speak. They mean the set of subconscious rules we actually use in formulating phrases and sentences of speech. In this sense, there is no such thing as bad grammar as far as linguistics is concerned. There are just many different languages and dialects whose grammars differ from each other to a greater or lesser extent. When linguists discuss grammars, they consider them to be psychologically real. That is, when they say, for example, that there is a rule for forming the plural in English which is 'Add an *s*', this is actually a hypothesis that somewhere in the brain of English speakers there is a neural network which carries out this procedure. So a grammar is really a set of hypotheses about the brain.

Grammars have several parts. **Phonology** is the set of rules about how sounds can and cannot be put together in a language. For example, *brick* is a perfectly good English word, whereas *btick* is not possible. This is because the rules about which sounds can go together in English do not allow two heavy consonants like *b* and *t* to go together at the beginning of a syllable. These phonological rules can differ somewhat from language to language. The word *pterodactyl* is pronounced as written in Greek, where sequences of consonants are allowed. In English, though, such sequences are not allowed, so when we adopted the Greek word, it was pronounced *terodactyl*. Sequences that are allowed by the grammar are called **grammatical**; those that are not allowed are called **ungrammatical**. The convention in linguistics is to mark ungrammatical sequences with an asterisk, as in *\*btick*.

**Morphology** is the part of the grammar that deals with the structure of words. Rules like 'Add *s* to make the plural' are morphological rules. **Syntax** deals with the rules that govern the way individual words are put together into sentences. For example, in English, sentences (2a) and (2b) below are grammatical and (2c) is not, because of the syntactic rules of the language.

(2)  (a)  The cat sat on the mat.

    (b)  On the mat sat the cat.

    (c)  *The cat sat the mat on.

You can often guess the meaning of sentences that violate syntactic rules, from the context and the words used, but you have a strong intuition that they are not quite right nonetheless. **Semantics** is the part of linguistics that deals with meaning. Meaning and grammaticality are two rather separate things. For example, in (3), one of the sentences is syntactically fine, but meaningless, at least if taken literally, whilst the other is ungrammatical, but has a clear meaning.

(3)  (a)  Colourless green ideas sleep furiously.

    (b)  The man wanted going to the cinema.

◈   In example (3), which sentence is ungrammatical and which is meaningless?

◆   Sentence (3a) is meaningless (how can something be colourless and green? how can an idea sleep, especially in a furious manner?), but nonetheless is put together just like a grammatical English sentence. Sentence (3b) seems to mean something like 'The man wanted to go to the cinema' or 'The man wanted taking to the cinema', but we know that it is not a good sentence.

Grammatical rules often involve classes of words. The key classes are **nouns** and **verbs**. Nouns typically denote objects. *Book*, *chair*, *man*, *cloud* and *water* are all nouns. Verbs typically denote actions or processes. *Go*, *come*, *ask*, *eat*, *harass* are all verbs. Verbs have a **subject**, the person or thing doing the action, and they may have an **object**, the person or thing to which the action is done. A verb with no object is called intransitive. *To sleep* is an intransitive verb, since you can say *I slept* but not *\*I slept the man*. *To kick* is a transitive verb, since you don't just kick in general, you kick someone or something.

◈   Can you think of any exceptions to the generalization that nouns denote objects and verbs denote actions or processes?

◆   Nouns like *arrival*, *explosion* and *assault* seem to denote actions or processes rather than objects.

Note that nouns such as arrival, explosion and assault are derived from verbs, in this case *to arrive*, *to explode*, *to assault*. They are called verbal nouns. The verb *to be* doesn't really describe a process; in fact, it doesn't really have any meaning of its own, but instead is used to join words together in a neutral way, as in *I am tall*.

As well as nouns and verbs, there are other, less important categories of words, such as adjectives, adverbs and prepositions.

•   Adjectives modify nouns to give us more information about their properties. Colour words are adjectives, as in 'the *green* man' or 'the *black* cat'.

•   Adverbs modify verbs, giving us more information about how the action was done, as in 'he arrived *stealthily*' or 'she shouted *loudly*'.

•   Prepositions and conjunctions are the little linking words that connect everything together, like *to*, *with*, *on*, *for*, *under*, *but*, *however* and *and*.

◆ For each of the following sentences, identify the nouns and verbs. Say whether the verb is transitive or intransitive, and identify the subject and object.

(4) (a) The man kicked the ball.

(b) The boy sulked.

(c) The dog ran after the cat with the attitude problem.

◆ (a) *Man* and *ball* are nouns, *kicked* is the verb. The verb is transitive. The subject is *the man* and the object is *the ball*.

(b) *Boy* is a noun and the verb is *sulked*. The verb is intransitive, with *the boy* as its subject.

(c) *Dog*, *cat* and *attitude problem* are nouns. The verb is *ran after*, which is transitive. *The dog* is the subject and *the cat with the attitude problem* is the object.

## 2.2.2   Generativity and duality of patterning

Let us now reconsider the sentence you heard in the imaginary scenario at the beginning of this chapter. Here it is again.

(1)   My dad's tutor's no joker, and he told me the TMA's going to hit home with a bang.

### Activity 2.2

Before reading this section, try writing down what stages you think the brain might go through in turning the sound of sentence (1) into its meaning. Think about what it is that makes the tasks difficult.

The vervet monkey call system, as we saw, involves a mapping between sounds and meanings, just as human language does. However, it differs from human language in two crucial respects. The first of these is called **generativity**. The three major vervet calls – *snake*, *leopard* and *eagle* – are meaningful units in their own right; you don't need to say anything else, you just call. The calls cannot be combined into higher-order complexes of meaning. A snake call followed by a leopard call could, as far as we understand it, express only the presence of a snake and a leopard. It could not express the proposition that a snake was at that moment being hunted by a leopard, or vice versa, or the idea that leopards are really much more of a nuisance than snakes. This means that the number of meanings expressible in the vervet system is closed, or finite. There are only as many meanings as there are calls. Human languages, by contrast, allow the recombination of their words into infinitely many arrangements, which have systematically different meanings by virtue of the way they are arranged.

In the vervet system, the monkeys can simply store in their memory the meaning associated with each call. Human language could not work this way. Consider example sentence (1) above. You have almost certainly never heard or read this exact sentence before. In fact, it is highly unlikely that anyone, in the entire history of humanity, has ever uttered this exact sentence before me today. Yet we all understand what it means. We must therefore all possess some machinery for making up new meanings out of smaller parts in real time. This is what is known as the **generative** capacity of language; the ability to make new meanings by recombining units. The vervet system is not generative, whereas human language is.

Vervet calls are indivisible wholes; they cannot be analysed as being made up of smaller units. Words, by contrast can be broken down into smaller sound units. Thus language exhibits what is known as **duality of patterning** (Figure 2.2). At the lowest level, there is a finite number of significant sounds, or **phonemes**. The exact number varies from language to language, but is generally in the range of a few dozen. The phonemes can be combined into words fairly freely; however there are restrictions, known as phonological rules, about how phonemes can go together. Words in their turn combine into sentences. However, as we have just said, not all combinations of words are grammatical. Which combinations are allowed depends on syntactic rules.

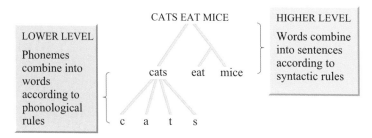

**Figure 2.2**   The two levels of patterning in human language.

There are some differences between the higher and lower levels of patterning in language. Phonemes, the basic unit of the lower level, have no meaning at all, whereas words, the basic unit of the higher level, typically carry meaning. The meaning of the word *bed* has nothing at all to do with the fact that the phonemes making it up are /b/, /e/ and /d/. If you change one phoneme, for example the /d/ to a /t/, then you have a word that is not just different but completely unrelated in meaning – *bet*. You could imagine a hypothetical linguistic system in which particular phonemes had special relationships to meanings; for example, in which words for furniture all began with /b/, or words for body parts all contained an /i/. No human language is like that, however. You cannot predict the meaning of a word, even in the vaguest terms, from the phonemes that make it up.

The / / notation is explained in Box 2.1.

The higher level of patterning is quite different. The meaning of a sentence *is* largely a product of the meanings of the individual words that it contains. Syntactic rules serve to identify which word in the sentence plays which role, and also to 'glue together' the relationships between the words. Consider these examples.

(5)   The cat bit the dog.

(6)   The cat which was bitten by the dog was thirsty.

In (5), we know that the cat was the biter and the dog the bitten because of a pattern in English syntax which says that the first noun is generally the subject of the sentence. In (6), there are two possible participants to which the state 'thirsty' could be attached – the dog could be thirsty or the cat could be thirsty. The syntax tells us that it must be the cat. Without syntax, no-one would be able to tell who was biting, who was bitten, and who was thirsty in (5) and (6), however much they knew about the behaviour of cats and dogs.

You might say that there is nothing that remarkable about understanding a sentence of spoken English. You listen out for the phonemes; as they come in, you store them in short-term memory until you have enough to make a word. Then the word is passed on to the meaning centres of the brain, where its meaning is activated, and the phonemes making up the next word start coming through. You continue this process until the whole sentence is in. You use your knowledge of syntax to clear up any uncertainties about who did what to whom, and there you are: the meaning. Simple really.

This account underestimates the crucial complexity of linguistic processing in several ways. We will explore this complexity by considering in detail how a sentence (sentence (1) from the opening of this chapter) could be understood. We will see that there are three areas of really difficult problems that the brain's linguistic system solves effortlessly. These are the phonological problem, the semantic problem, and the syntactic problem.

### 2.2.3    From ear to phoneme: the phonological problem

The phonological problem is the problem of knowing which units (words, calls) are being uttered. The speech signal is a pattern of sound, and sound consists of patterns of minute vibrations in the air. Sounds vary in their frequency distribution. The sound of a flute playing is relatively **harmonic**. This means that the energy of the sound is concentrated at certain frequencies of vibration. A plot of the energy of a sound against the frequency at which that energy occurs is called a spectrogram. A spectrogram for a flute's note is shown in Figure 2.3a. As you can see there are slim coloured bands, and black spaces in between. The coloured bands are the regions of the frequency spectrum where the acoustic energy is concentrated, whereas in the black areas there is little or no acoustic energy. The lowest coloured band corresponds to the **fundamental frequency** of the sound. This is where the most energy is concentrated, and it is the fundamental frequency which gives the sensation of the pitch of the sound. The higher bands are called the **formant frequencies**. In a 'pure' tone, their frequencies are mathematical multiples of the fundamental (in acoustics in general, they are also called overtones or harmonics, but in relation to speech, they are always called formants). The relative strengths of the different formants determine the timbre or texture of the sound.

**Figure 2.3**   Spectrogram of (a) a single note from a flute; and (b) a box being dropped on the floor. Black represents no acoustic energy at a given frequency. The 'hotter' the colour (i.e. towards the red or yellow end of the spectrum), the greater the concentration of energy at that frequency. Note in (a) that the greatest concentration of energy is in the lowest band (the fundamental frequency), with regular and increasingly faint harmonics at higher frequencies. The harmonics have clear gaps between them, which creates the feeling of a pure and tuneful note. In (b), by contrast, the acoustic energy is smeared across the whole frequency range, making it sound like a noise rather than a note.

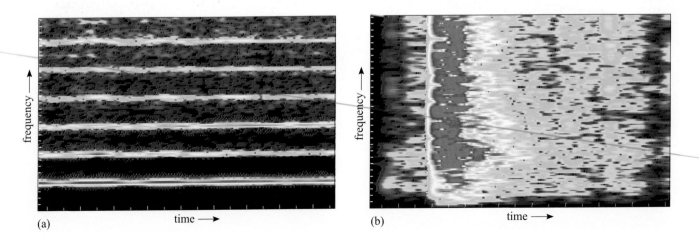

(a)    time ⟶

(b)    time ⟶

◆ In terms of fundamental and formant frequencies, why might a violin, a flute, an oboe and a human voice producing the same note sound so different?

◆ The fundamental frequency is necessarily the same in all cases, since the pitch of the note is the same. The relative strength of the different formants is the main source of the different qualities – thin, reedy, soft, full or whatever – of the notes.

In contrast to harmonic sounds are sounds in which the acoustic energy is dispersed across the frequency spectrum, like the box being dropped in Figure 2.3b. These are experienced as noises rather than tones (it is impossible to hum them), and they appear on the spectrogram as a smear of colour.

For the vervet monkeys, the phonological problem is not too difficult. There are only three major alarm calls, and their acoustic shapes are radically different and non-overlapping (Figure 2.4). They are also different from the other vocalizations vervets produce during social encounters. Thus the incoming signal has to be analysed and matched to a stored representation of one of the three calls.

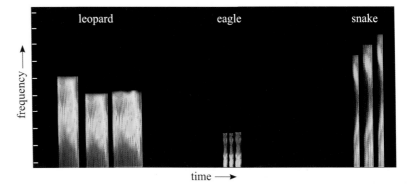

**Figure 2.4** Spectrogram of the three vervet alarm calls.

The human case is more complex. The first stage is to extract which phonemes are being uttered. Phonemes come in two major classes, consonants and vowels. **Vowels** are harmonic sounds. They are produced by periodic vibration of the vocal folds which in turn causes the vibration of air molecules. The frequency of this vibration determines the pitch (fundamental frequency) of the sound. Different vowels differ in quality, or timbre, and the different qualities are made by changing the shape of the resonating space in front of the vocal folds, by moving the position of the lips and tongue relative to the teeth and palate. This produces different spectrogram shapes, as shown in Figure 2.5. (The conventions used in this chapter to represent spoken language are given in Box 2.1.)

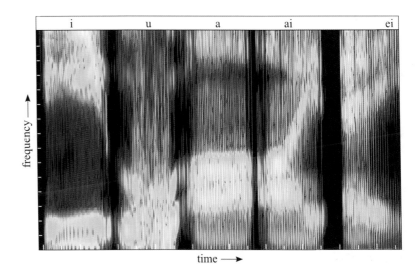

**Figure 2.5** The spectrogram shapes of five vowels, spoken by the author. The vowels correspond to the vowel sounds in *beat*, *boot*, *bet*, *bite* and *bait*. What distinguishes the different vowels is not the absolute frequency of the formants but their position relative to each other.

## Box 2.1    Representing spoken language

The spelling we usually use to represent English in text does not relate very systematically to the sounds we actually make. Consider, for example, the words farm and pharmacy. The beginnings of the words are identical to the ear, and yet they are written using different letters. The reasons for this are usually historical, in this case due to pharmacy coming into English from Greek. The letter r is also there as a historical remnant – the r in farm is now silent, but it used to be pronounced, and still is in some varieties of English, for example in South-West England and in Scotland.

For linguists it matters what sounds people actually produce, so they often represent spoken language using a system called the International Phonetic Alphabet (IPA). Sequences of speech transcribed in IPA are enclosed in slash brackets, / /, or square brackets, [ ], to distinguish them from ordinary text. Many of the letters of the IPA have more or less the same value as conventional English spelling. For example, /s/, /t/, /d/ and /l/ represent the sounds that you would expect. The IPA is always consistent about the representation of sounds, so cat and kitten are both transcribed as beginning with a /k/.

The full IPA makes use of quite a lot of specialized symbols and distinctions that are beyond our purposes here, so we have used ordinary letters but tried to make the representation of words closer to what is actually said wherever this is relevant to the argument. We have used the convention of slash brackets to indicate wherever we have done this, so for example, the word cat would be /kat/ and sugar would be /shuga/.

◇ Is the vowel of *bit* higher or lower in pitch than the vowel of *bat*?

◆ There is no inherent difference in pitch (fundamental frequency) between *bit* and *bat*. You can demonstrate this by saying either of them in either a deep or a high pitched voice. The difference between them is in the relative position of the higher formant frequencies.

The relative position of the first two formant frequencies is crucial for vowel recognition. Artificial speech using just two formants is comprehensible, though in real speech there are higher formants too. These higher formants reflect idiosyncracies of the vocal tract, and thus are very useful in recognizing the identity of the speaker and the emotional colouring of the speech. Some of the vowels of English have a simple flat formant shape, like the /a/ and /i/ in Figure 2.5. Others, like the vowels of *bite* and *bait*, involve a pattern of formant movement. Vowels where the formants move relative to each other are called diphthongs.

**Consonants**, in contrast to vowels, are not generally harmonic sounds. Vowels are made by the vibration of the vocal folds resonated through the throat and mouth with the mouth at least partly open. Consonants, by contrast, are the various scrapes, clicks and bangs made by closing some part of the throat, tongue or lips for a moment.

◆ Make a series of different consonants sandwiched between two vowels – *apa*, *ata*, *aka*, *ava*, *ama*, *afa*, *ada*, *aga*, *a'a* (like the Cockney way of saying *butter*). Where is the point of closure in each case and what is brought to closure against what?

◆ *apa, ama*   The two lips together

   *ata, ada*   The tip of the tongue against the ridge behind the back of the top teeth

   *aka, aga*   The back of the tongue against the roof of the mouth at the back

   *ava, afa*   The bottom lip against the top teeth

   *a'a*        The glottis (opening at the back of the throat) closing

The acoustics of the consonants are rather varied. Some consonants produce a burst of broad spectrum noise – look for instance at the /sh/ in Figure 2.6. Others have relatively little acoustic energy of their own, and are most detectable by the way they affect the onset of the formants of the following vowel.

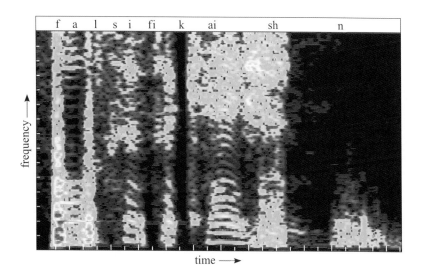

frequency ⟶

time ⟶

**Figure 2.6**   Spectrogram of the word *falsification* spoken by the author. Note the period of silence (black areas) in the word. This corresponds to the closure during the formation of the /k/ sound. The /sh/ corresponds to a burst of noise over most of the spectrum.

Phonemes make up small groups called syllables. Typically a syllable will be one consonant followed by one vowel, like *me*, *you* or *we*. Sometimes, though, the syllable will contain more consonants, as in *them* or *string*. Different languages allow different syllable shapes, from Hawai'ian which only tolerates alternating consonants and vowels (which we can represent as CVCVCV), to languages like Polish which seem to us to have heavy clusters of consonant sounds. English is somewhere in the middle, allowing things like *bra* and *sta* but not allowing other combinations like *\*tsa* or *\*pta*.

◆ Pause for thought: Why do you think language might employ a basic structure of CVCVCV?

◆ Long strings of consonants are impossible for the hearer to discriminate, since identification of some consonants depend upon the deflection they cause to the formants of the following vowel. Long strings of vowels merge into each other. Consonants help break up the string of vowels into discrete chunks. So an alternation of the two kinds of sound is an optimal arrangement – after all, the babbling of a baby uses it.

The task of identifying phonemes in real speech is made difficult by two factors. The first is the problem of *variation*. Phonemes might seem categorically different to us, but that is the product of our brain's activity, not the actual acoustic situation. Vowels differ from each other only by degree, and this is also true for many consonants. A continuum can be set up between a clear /ba/ and a clear /da/ (Figure 2.7). Listening to computer-generated sounds along this continuum, the hearer hears absolutely /ba/ up to a certain point, then absolutely /da/, with only a small zone of uncertainty in between. In that zone of uncertainty (and to some extent outside it), the context will tend to determine what is heard. What the listener does not experience is a sound with some /ba/ properties and some /da/ properties. It is heard as either one or the other, an effect known as **categorical perception**.

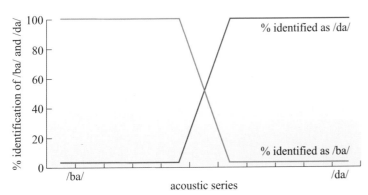

**Figure 2.7**  Categorical perception of /ba/ versus /da/ as a function of change in a computer-generated speech signal. The signal is varied continuously in a linear fashion, but what the hearer hears is a non-linear change; /ba/ until a certain point, where after the sound quite suddenly becomes /da/.

The hearer cannot rely on the absolute frequency of formants to identify vowels, since, as we have seen, you can pronounce any vowel at any pitch, and different speakers have different depths of voices. So a transformation must be performed to extract the position of (at least) the first two formants relative to the fundamental frequency. But that is not all; different dialects have slightly different typical positions of formants of each vowel; within dialects, different speakers have slightly different typical positions; and worst of all, within speakers, the relative positions of the formants change a little from utterance to utterance of the same underlying vowel (Figure 2.8). The hearer thus needs to make a best guess from very messy data.

This is made more difficult by the second factor, which is called **co-articulation**. The realization of a phoneme depends on the phonemes next to it. The /b/ of *bat* is not quite the same, acoustically, as the /b/ of *bit*. We are so good at hearing phonemes as phonemes that it is difficult to consciously perceive that this is so, except by taking an extreme example, as in the exercise below.

◆ Listen closely to the phoneme /n/ in your own pronunciation of the word *ten*, in the following three contexts – *ten newts, ten kings, ten men*. Say the words repeatedly but naturally to identify the precise qualities of the /n/ in each case. Are they the same? If not what has happened to them?

◆ You will probably find that the articulation of the /n/ is 'dragged around' by the following consonant – towards the /ng/ of *long* in *ten kings*, and towards /m/ in *ten men*. If this is not clear, try saying *ten men tem men* over and over again (or alternatively *ten kings teng kings*). You soon realize that there is no acoustic difference whatever between the two phrases. This is an example of assimilation, a closely related phenomenon to co-articulation.

Co-articulation makes the task of the hearer even harder, because they have to undo the co-articulation that the speaker has put in (unavoidably, since co-articulation is unstoppable in fast connected speech). A sound which is identical to an /m/ which the listener has previously heard might actually be an /m/, but it might equally be an /n/ with co-articulation induced by the context. An upward curving onset to a vowel might signal a /d/ if the vowel is /e/, but a /b/ if the vowel is /a/. Yet the listener

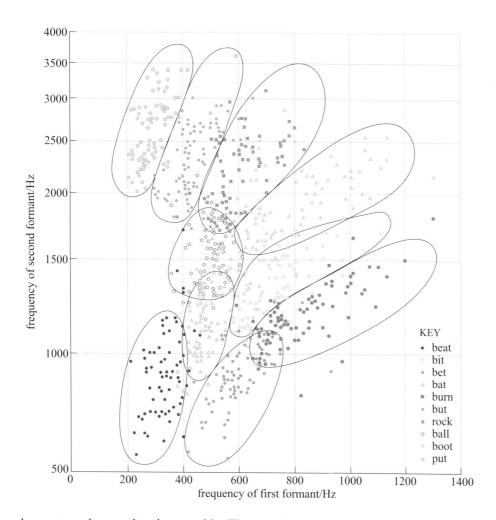

**Figure 2.8** Acoustic realization of different English vowels in samples of normal speech from several speakers. The graph shows the first and second formants of the vowel sound from the different words shown in the key. Note that the vertical scale is not linear.

does not yet know what the vowel is. They are having to identify the signal under multiple and simultaneous uncertainties. Speakers use their expectations about what is to follow to resolve these uncertainties.

Other problems arise in the extraction of words from sound. Consider Figure 2.9, which is part of the spectrogram of the author producing sentence (1). Our brains so effortlessly segment speech into words that we are tempted to assume that the breaks between the words are 'out there' in the signal. But as you can see, there are no such gaps in speech. There are moments of low acoustic intensity (black areas), but they do not necessarily coincide with word boundaries. Co-articulation of phonemes can cross word boundaries.

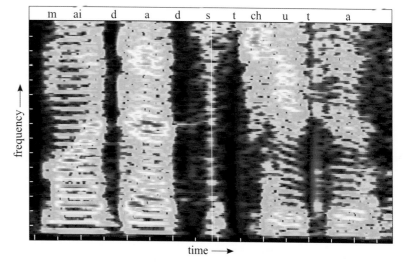

**Figure 2.9** Spectrogram of the phrase *my dad's tutor*, spoken by the author.

Strings of phonemes have multiple possible segmentations. *My dad's tutor* could be segmented, among many other possibilities, as:

(7)  (a)  [my] [dads] [tu] [tor]

     (b)  [mide] [ad] [stewt] [er]

     (c)  [mida] [dstu] [tor]

The signal rarely contains the key explicitly. The hearer can exploit knowledge of English phonological rules, for example to exclude (7c) on the grounds that it contains an impossible English syllable. Beyond that, knowledge of words must come into play. Segmentation (7b) is phonotactically fine, but doesn't mean anything in English. Our segmentations always alight on those solutions that furnish a string of real words, so (7a) would be chosen. If your name was (7b), you would have extreme trouble introducing yourself, however clearly you spoke, whereas any segmentation containing whole words is much easier to understand.

◆   Can you see any problems that might arise with achieving either phoneme identification before segmentation into words, or segmentation into words before phoneme identification?

◆   As we saw above, identification of phonemes often depends upon the word context. On the other hand, segmentation into words depends upon identifying the phonemes. In short it seems likely that neither can always be achieved prior to the other.

We will consider models of how the brain actually does it in the second half of this chapter.

### 2.2.4   From phoneme to meaning: the semantic problem

For a vervet monkey, once an alarm call has been assigned to the correct phonological class – *leopard*, *snake* or *eagle* – then the task is straightforward indeed. Each of these sound patterns is connected in long-term memory to some 'prototype' of the predator in question, including what it looks like, what it does and so on. The *eagle* call always means eagle, whatever the context. The activation of the brain trace for the *eagle* call invariably activates the brain trace for the eagle meaning. That is how the monkeys know to look up after an eagle call and down after a snake call.

The classic way of describing language processing in psychology textbooks makes it seem that human language is not much different. Each word, these textbooks say, is linked to a non-linguistic 'prototype' of what it means. For *eagle*, this would be pretty similar to the vervet's representation of the *eagle* call's meaning. The trouble with this account is that much of the meaning in human language is not really like that.

Many words in everyday language do not carry any meaning, at least not in anything like the *eagle* sense. Consider sentence (8).

(8)  It is raining.

There is only one element in (8) with any independent meaning. The *it* certainly does not refer to anything. (You can't seek clarification of (8) by asking *What is raining?*) The *is* has no meaning. Indeed, the verb *to be* in general is completely devoid of intrinsic meaning. So why are there three words in this sentence, which really consists of a single meaningful element – *raining*?

Many words in language are there only because the syntax of a language demands that sentences conform to certain templates; in English, for example, that they have both a verb and a subject. The subject is usually the doer in a sentence. But there is no real subject in the fact that it is raining today – it is just a state of affairs. Thus English syntax demands we fill in the sentence with what is largely meaningless material – *it* – to make the sentence well-formed. Italian, which is more relaxed about the overt expression of a subject, allows example (8) to be captured with a single word (9), which is also a well-formed sentence.

(9)  Piove.

Other languages, like Hebrew and Arabic, relax the requirement for every sentence to have a verb, allowing sentences like (10).

(10) Anii ayaf.

> I tired (masculine).

> I am tired.

However they differ, languages all require a wealth of material whose meaning is either nearly zero, or is filled in entirely from context. Thus for some words, what you look up in long-term memory is not a prototype of the thing to which the word refers, but a further instruction to look for something else in the sentence. Inferring which function a word is carrying in a sentence is subtle. Consider (11).

(11) (a)  Paula and Mary ran panting in from the field, where the dog was barking. It was running now.

(b)  Paula and Mary ran panting in from the field, where the dog was barking. It was ploughed now.

(c)  Paula and Mary ran panting in from the field, where the dog was barking. It was raining now.

These sentence pairs differ only by a single word. In (11a), *it* is generally taken to mean the dog. In (11b), the *it* cannot be read as identifying the dog; it must mean the field. In (11c), the *it* stands for neither dog nor field, but is a purely syntactic *it* filled in by the need for the verb to have a subject. Thus, having identified *it* as the word spoken in this position in the sentence, the brain has to try out several possibilities for its meaning in the context, until it comes up with one that makes some kind of sense. Note that you cannot begin to work out what the *it* means in (11) until you have had the key word *running*, *ploughed* or *raining*. This is a very important point. In processing language in general, you cannot process the meaning of all the elements in the order in which they come. Consider (12).

(12) (a)  As they crashed into the bank, the robbers leapt from their car.

(b)  As they crashed into the bank, the men leapt from their canoe.

The meaning of *bank* could be to do with money or to do with rivers. This cannot be resolved until later information arrives. *Bank* must thus be kept in a pending tray somewhere until more data are available. Linguists thus believe the brain must have a storage pad in which sentences are assembled and disassembled, with the words represented in a way which is still neutral as to which meaning is the right one.

Thus, identifying the meaning of a word depends not just on the phonological form of the word, but on two other things. These are the rest of the sentence, and also the wider context of the discourse. This latter is important, since your reading of (12b) would be quite different in a story about three guys who decide to rob Barclays disguised as the British kayaking team on a promotional tour.

The resolution of meaning depends on a dynamic interplay of these three elements. Often the meaning of a set of words departs almost entirely from the meaning you would expect from them individually. Just consider example (1). It has nothing to do with hitting, nothing to do with homes, and only a very metaphorical bang. Sentences as least as complex as this are everyday occurrences, yet you decode their meanings in a completely automatic way without even being aware of the work your brain is having to do.

## 2.2.5   From phoneme to sentence structure: the syntactic problem

In the vervet monkey system, calls stand by themselves. Thus there is no syntax. Syntax can be thought of as working like road traffic rules do. It doesn't much matter which side of the road you drive on, as long as there is some clear convention. Similarly in (13), it is necessary to understand the difference between (13a) and (13b) without ambiguity, by having some rule or other about which noun phrase comes first. England may differ from most of the rest of the world in terms of the side of the road that it drives on, but English agrees with 99% of all languages in the syntactic convention that the first noun phrase encountered is generally taken to be the subject.

(13) (a)  The cat bit the dog.

  (b)  The dog bit the cat.

Syntax is concerned with such problems as the assignment of roles (subject, object, etc.) to the different participants in a sentence, and the binding together of different meanings. The syntactic task involved in even a straightforward sentence is of fearsome complexity. Consider for example (14).

(14) (a)  The dog bit the green cat.

  (b)  The dog which bit the cat was green.

  (c)  The dog which bit the cat your uncle Marvin warned you would betray you on your fourteenth birthday was green.

In all these sentences, there are at least three important word meanings activated – *dog*, *cat* and *green*. We can assume that these meanings are different bundles of sensory features in long-term memory somewhere, which get activated by the recognition of their respective word forms. The question is how *green* gets hooked to the correct one of the other two traces, *dog* and *cat*. This is known as the **binding problem**. (This is the same general issue as the binding problem of Book 1, Section 4.2.2.) How the brain solves the binding problem is an active area of research.

You might assume from (14a) that knowing which bindings to make in language was quite straightforward. The brain, encountering an adjective, just has to look for the nearest noun phrase, and bind the meanings together. Thus in (14a), green must be the cat not the dog because *green* is next to *cat*. However, in (14b), *green* is closest to *cat* in the sentence, but its meaning applies to the dog. In (14c), *green* is 17 words away from *dog*. After *dog* come several other things which could be green; the cat, you and uncle Marvin. However, the only possible sense of this sentence for any native speaker of English is that the dog is green.

This tells us some very significant things about syntactic processing. The first is that the binding of different words together depends not upon their linear position in the sentence, but on their underlying syntactic relationships. The processing of syntactic relations cannot be completed until the whole sentence is finished.

The brain's analysis of sentences depends upon identifying key words, which then offer 'slots' into which to bind the meanings of other elements. Thus in (14a), the verb *bit* offers two slots for noun phrases to bind to, one for the subject and one for the object. Any noun phrase which precedes the verb binds into the subject position. The first noun in a noun phrase is the head noun; the head noun offers slots to which other words like adjectives and articles (*green* and *the*) can bind. A whole clause can bind onto a head noun – this is what happens in (14c), where the clause *which bit the cat ... birthday* binds to *the dog*. The whole thing then becomes a super-noun phrase which binds as a whole into the subject position of *bit* – that is, the subject of *bit* is not strictly *the dog* but *the dog which bit the cat ... birthday*. Another way of looking at the non-binding of *green* to *the cat* is to say that *the cat* is already bound (into a noun phrase) and so is not free to go hooking up with verbs that might be floating around.

There are many other subtle syntactic processes, most of which we cannot consider here. Consider (1) again.

(1)   My dad's tutor's no joker, and he told me the TMA's going to hit home with a bang.

The brain has to assign a value to the *he*. It could be *my dad* that told me, or it could be *my dad's tutor*. The phrase *with a bang* could modify the way the TMA is going to hit home, or it could modify the way I was told about it. The former interpretation is preferred, but if you changed it to *with a smile*, then your interpretation flips to the latter. This is a case where the semantics of a word informs the syntactic analysis of the sentence.

Overall, then, the brain attempts to bind the words that the phonology has identified into a syntactic package that is well-formed, and liaises with the semantics to see if a sensible meaning is thereby produced. This is a dynamic process, with interaction in real-time between the different components, which finally crystallizes on a unique meaning for at least most sentences. It is many orders of magnitude more complex than the vervet system, or indeed any other cognitive system that has yet been described. We will consider in Section 2.3 how the brain does it.

## Summary of Section 2.2

Human language is a complex communication system that allows the generation of infinitely many different messages by combining the basic sounds (phonemes) into words, and combining the words into larger units called sentences. The way the sounds combine is governed by phonological rules, and the way the words combine is governed by syntactic rules.

Phonemes can be divided into the vowels, which are made by vibration of the vocal folds, and consonants, which are abrupt sounds made by bringing two surfaces in the vocal tract together. Different phonemes have different acoustic shapes, but in connected speech these are variable because of the influence of the sounds before and after (co-articulation), so the hearer has to make a best guess using information from the context.

The meaning of a sentence is more complex than just the sum of the meanings of the words in the sentence. The hearer must also perform a syntactic analysis of the sentence to establish which meanings relate to which others, and to fill in elements that are ambiguous. The syntactic relationships within a sentence are not simply reflected by the order in which the words arrive, so the hearer has to keep the sentence in a working memory buffer whilst different interpretations are tried out, in order to come up with one that is both grammatical and meaningful.

## 2.3    The brain's solution: the machinery of language

Now that we have examined the processes involved in understanding a sentence in some detail, we will turn to the issue of how the brain achieves the task. We will begin with the initial capture and analysis of the speech signal.

### 2.3.1    Speech perception

Vibrations in the air are channelled by the structure of the external ear into the ear canal (Figure 2.10). (We looked at the internal structure of the ear in Book 4, Figure 3.11.) In the middle ear, they encounter a taut membrane or eardrum stretched across the ear canal. The vibrations in the air set up sympathetic vibrations in the eardrum. Inside the middle ear is a set of three tiny bones, the **auditory ossicles**. The auditory ossicles in their turn are caused to vibrate by the vibrations of the eardrum. The inner end of the auditory ossicles abuts a fluid-filled coiled structure called the **cochlea**. Vibration of the ossicles is transferred into the fluid of the cochlea and particularly into a thin membrane that runs along its length called the **basilar membrane**. Adjacent to the basilar membrane is a layer of small receptor cells, each with tiny cilia or hairs on it. Indeed, these receptors are known as **hair cells** (Figure 2.11). Movement of the basilar membrane causes movement of the hairs, which is converted into changes in electrical activity within the cell. Hair cells form synaptic connections with adjacent neurons, and thus electrical changes within them trigger neuronal action potentials. These neurons join into the **auditory nerve**, which relays the action potentials from the ear to the brain.

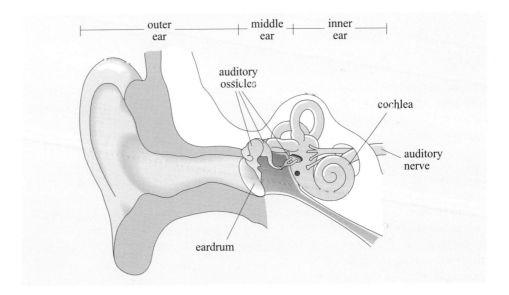

**Figure 2.10**    A cutaway diagram of the human ear.

The pattern of vibration of the eardrum and ossicles is simply a reflection of the pattern of vibration in the air. In the cochlea, transformation of the signal begins. Because of the structure of the cochlea, high-frequency vibrations cause displacement of the basilar membrane at the outer end, and low-frequency vibrations cause displacement further along. Thus different hair cells at different positions will respond to different frequencies of sound, by virtue of being adjacent to different sections of the basilar membrane.

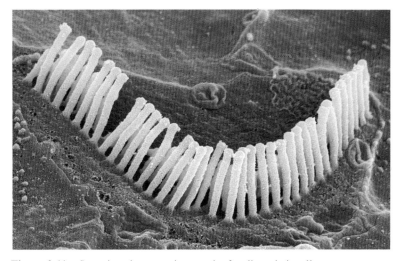

**Figure 2.11**   Scanning electron micrograph of auditory hair cells.

Thus, two crucial things have happened at the cochlear stage. First, a mapping of sounds of different frequencies onto different places on the basilar membrane has been set up. This is called **tonotopic** organization. Second, any sound which consists of patterns of acoustic energy at several different frequencies will have been broken down into its component frequencies. This is because each formant within the complex sound will cause vibration at a different position along the basilar membrane and hence cause different subsets of hair cells to respond. Action potentials generated in the neurons that connect to the hair cells are transmitted to the brain via the auditory nerve. What will be transmitted to the brain, then, already contains information about pitch (coded by which cells are firing), and a preliminary breakdown into formants.

The auditory nerve feeds into the brainstem (at the cochlear nucleus), from where the auditory pathway ascends into the medial geniculate nucleus of the thalamus, the relay station in the middle of the forebrain (Figure 2.12). The main route for auditory information from here is to the auditory cortex of the superior temporal lobe on both sides of the brain (though there is also another pathway to the amygdala, not shown on the figure). Neurons in the auditory cortex generally respond to information from the ear on the opposite side of the body, though some integration of information from the two ears occurs at the brainstem level.

Representation of the signal in the primary auditory cortex is tonotopic. That is, cells at different locations respond to sounds at different frequencies,

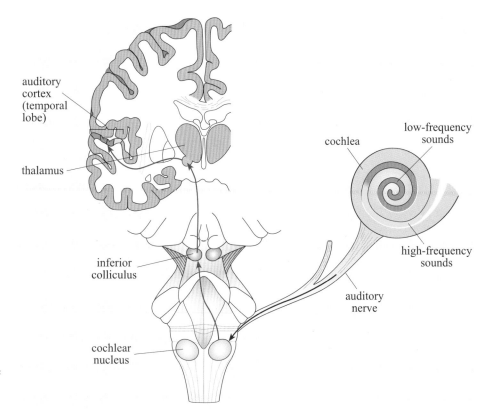

**Figure 2.12**   Connections from the ear to the primary auditory cortex. The arrow indicates the route of the auditory information.

**Figure 2.13** Tonotopic organization within the primary auditory cortex.

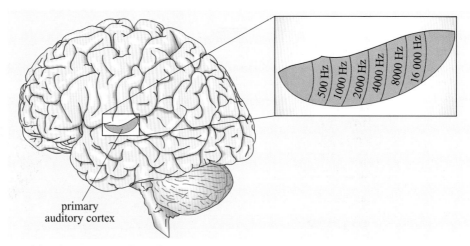

primary auditory cortex

resulting in a 'map' of the frequency spectrum of the sound laid out across the surface of the brain (Figure 2.13). Recognition of sounds depends not on the absolute pitch of the formants but on their relationship to each other. We assume that this is processed in deeper layers of the auditory cortex, though exactly where or how is not yet understood.

There is some evidence that within the primary auditory cortex, there are populations of neurons specialized for speech. This was shown by brain imaging experiments that compared patterns of activation in response to speech, scrambled cocktails of speech sounds, and non-speech sounds which were matched to the speech sounds on basic acoustic features (Moore, 2000). Areas in the superior temporal sulcus, on both sides of the brain, responded preferentially to real and scrambled speech (Figure 2.14), rather than to the other sounds.

Listening to speech produces activation on both sides of the brain in the auditory cortex. Damage to the superior temporal lobe on either side causes difficulties with speech recognition, though the pattern of the difficulties may be somewhat different on the two sides.

Thus it seems that the initial perception of speech is processed by some of the neurons in the auditory areas of the superior temporal lobe, on both sides of the brain. As we have seen, though, there is a great deal more to language than identifying phonemes and formants; similarly, there are many more brain areas which, when damaged, cause problems with speech and language. We must thus consider the architecture of the whole language processing system.

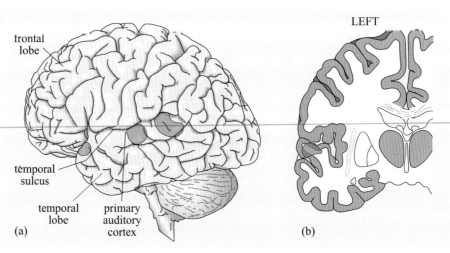

LEFT

frontal lobe

temporal sulcus

temporal lobe

primary auditory cortex

(a)

(b)

**Figure 2.14**   Cortical areas that respond preferentially to speech or scrambled speech sounds, as opposed to non-speech sounds. (a) Lateral view, (b) coronal section.

66

## 2.3.2   The anatomy of the language system

Perhaps the best-known generalization about the language system is that it is represented on one side of the brain – usually the left – more than the other. Many lines of evidence support this view. Specific impairments to linguistic abilities are known as **aphasia**, and aphasia results much more often from damage to the left hemisphere of the brain than from damage to the right. It is also possible to temporarily deactivate one or other hemisphere. This is usually done as an investigative prelude to brain surgery, particularly in cases of epilepsy. It can be done by injecting a fast-acting drug into the carotid artery on one side of the body, or alternatively by weak electrical stimulation of part of the cortex. (This technique was introduced in Book 3, Section 2.4.1.) Deactivation of the left hemisphere causes a disruption of speech and language much more often than does deactivation of the right hemisphere. These techniques have also led to estimates that language is processed predominantly in the left hemisphere in about 97% of right-handed people but in about only 60% of left-handers.

We argued in the previous section that the initial perception of speech, like that of other sounds, was carried out bilaterally, whereas in this section we have argued that language is usually lateralized to the left hemisphere. There must thus be a point in the analysis of the speech signal where mechanisms on just one side 'take over' from the bilateral auditory areas. Brain scanning studies show that this is indeed the case: the additional activation in response to speech which is understood, compared to speech which is in an unknown language, is mainly on the left.

Further insight into such lateralization comes from 'split-brain' patients. These are people who, because of severe epilepsy, have had the corpus callosum, the bundle of fibres connecting the two hemispheres, cut. This means that there is no direct neural connection between the left and right hemispheres. In these individuals, stimuli presented to the right hand, right ear, and right side of the visual field will mainly be processed by the left hemisphere, and stimuli presented to the left-hand side are processed by the right hemisphere. Objects presented to the left hemisphere can be named and talked about, whereas those presented to the right hemisphere generally cannot.

The right hemisphere does have some linguistic abilities. In split-brain patients the left hand can reach out and choose an object whose name has been presented to the right hemisphere, just as the right hand can choose an object whose name has been presented to the left hemisphere. However, the right hand can also choose the drawing that illustrates a sentence like *The girl kisses the boy*, whereas the left hand cannot correctly discriminate this situation from one in which the boy kisses the girl. Similarly, the right hemisphere cannot identify the scenes represented by *The dog jumps over the fence* versus *The dogs jump over the fence*, and so on. Thus, right-hemisphere language ability is limited to the phonological analysis of individual words, and access to their concrete meanings; sentence processing is the pure province of the left.

The areas within the left hemisphere which are most important for speech and language have been identified by several lines of evidence. Post-mortem examination of the brains of people affected by aphasia identified two main areas which were most often damaged – one in the frontal lobe and one further back, in the temporal lobe, close to the junction of temporal and parietal lobes. These areas are known respectively as Broca's area and Wernicke's area, after the scientists who first identified their associations with language. Because of their respective positions, they are sometimes also called the anterior and posterior language areas. Evidence from

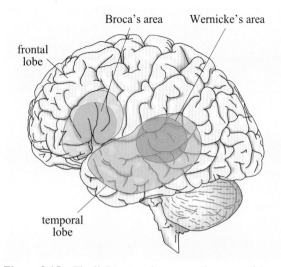

**Figure 2.15**   The lighter toned areas are the areas of the left hemisphere in which electrical stimulation disrupts speech and language. The two darker toned areas are Broca's and Wernicke's areas.

non-aphasic individuals generally supports the importance of these areas. In one procedure, the cerebral cortex can be weakly electrically stimulated, as a prelude to brain surgery for epilepsy. The patient can be awake during this procedure – since the brain contains no nociceptive neurons, only local anaesthesia is required. Thus, the patient can perform a verbal task whilst the electrical stimulation is moved around different areas of the brain.

Electrical stimulation disrupts speech and language activities mainly when it is on the left of the brain, and only in specific areas (Figure 2.15). These areas are in the general regions of Broca's and Wernicke's areas, as predicted. There is also an additional area in the left superior frontal lobe. This is in part of the cortex generally associated with motor functions, and may be important for the execution of speech production more than for language processing per se. There is also evidence for the involvement of tissues further down into the temporal lobe than the extension of the classical Wernicke's area/posterior language area. (Subcortical structures appear to be important, too, but they are beyond the scope of this chapter.)

Brain imaging studies support the map shown in Figure 2.15. Tasks to do with speech and language lead to increased regional blood flow – which is suggestive of greater neuronal 'work' – across a broad range of structures in the left hemisphere, generally within the triangle demarcated by Broca's and Wernicke's areas and the horn of the temporal lobe. There is strong evidence, which we will review in the next three sections, that this large area does not operate as an undifferentiated whole in the processing of language. Nor should we expect it to; as we saw in the first half of the chapter, decoding a sentence involves several distinct subtasks. The key questions to occupy researchers have thus been which subpart of the language cortex is associated with which subtask of overall language processing, and how does the processing of a sentence proceed in time through the various subareas and subtasks? The main lines of evidence we have to answer these questions come from three sources: aphasic patients, brain scanning, and electrophysiological studies. We will look at each of these in turn in the next three subsections.

### 2.3.3   Specialization within language areas: aphasia

Aphasia is caused by localized brain damage, for example due to a stroke or an automobile accident. General intellectual functioning is not necessarily impaired, as the person can still perform non-linguistic tasks. Nor is the understanding and production of language necessarily completely abolished. Instead, there are highly specific patterns of impairment in the way language is processed.

Aphasia is divided into two main types, fluent and non-fluent. For reasons which will become apparent, they are also known as Wernicke's and Broca's aphasia. In non-fluent, or Broca's aphasia, the person has a marked problem with speech production. Speech rate is slow, and the articulation of speech is laboured and distorted. Speech lacks its normal intonation contours, being instead pronounced in rather a monotonic way. The typical feel of non-fluent aphasic speech is given by a sample from a patient in (15). The patient was attempting to explain that he had come to the hospital for dental surgery. The dots indicate long pauses.

(15) Yes ... ah ... Monday ... er ... Dad and Peter H ... [his own name] and Dad ... er ... hospital ... and ah ... Wednesday ... Wednesday nine o'clock ... and oh ... Thursday ... ten o'clock, ah doctors ... two ... an doctors ... and er ... teeth ... yah

◈ Describe as specifically as possible the ways in which this sample of non-fluent aphasic language is similar to and differs from normal language use.

◆ In the sample, all the key referring words (the people involved, places and times, doctors, hospital and teeth) have been appropriately selected. Thus there is no apparent deficit in selecting the correct referring words on the basis of their meaning. These are all nouns, however; there are no verbs. More generally, there is no evidence of words being glued together into higher structures like sentences or phrases.

It was once thought that the comprehension abilities of people with non-fluent aphasia were normal. Thus, non-fluent aphasia was conceptualized as a disorder of language production that did not affect language comprehension. It is indeed the case that people with non-fluent aphasia can sometimes understand even quite complex sentences, in sharp contrast to what they produce. However, some subtle investigations over the last few decades have shown that language comprehension is also affected, and thus that the disorder is one of language in general, rather than just production (Berndt et al., 1997). Consider (16).

(16) (a) The dog chased the cat.

(b) The cat chased the dog.

(c) The girl watered the flowers.

(d) The flowers were watered by the girl.

(e) The dog was chased by the cat.

People with non-fluent aphasia can generally pick out the picture corresponding to (16a) or (16b) correctly. It might seem that the difference between (16a) and (16b) is purely syntactic; the words are after all the same in each case. Thus people with non-fluent aphasia seem able to use syntax in understanding if not in production. They can also correctly identify the picture associated with (16c) and (16d). Sentence (16d) is passive; this means that the usual generalization that the first thing you come across is the subject and the second one the object does not hold in this case. Again, the fact that people with non-fluent aphasia often get the right meaning suggests that they are using syntax. However, in (16a) to (16c), you can get the right meaning simply by assuming the first thing you come across is the agent or doer. In (16d), you can guess the correct meaning simply from the individual meanings of the words present; flowers can't water a girl, so the correct meaning has to be the other way around. Thus, you could get (16a) to (16d) correct without really using any sophisticated syntax, but just by general reasoning from the words present.

Sentence (16e) is different. Using the principle of subject first is a red herring, since it would lead you to assume that the dog was the chaser not the chased; and, unlike (16d), either assignment of roles is plausible. The only way you can tell which meaning is intended in (16e) is by applying a syntactic analysis. People with non-fluent aphasia are very bad at sentences like (16e). They tend to get the roles the wrong way around. In a similar way, non-fluent aphasics are fine with (17a), but bad with (17b).

(17) (a)  The man who pushed the woman is old.

(b)  The man who the woman pushed is old.

Once again, the explanation must be to do with syntax. In (17a), the subject of the verb *to push* is *the man*, which comes before the verb, so even though the sentence is moderately complex, the agent is coming first. In (17b), *the man* is the object of the verb *to push*; at some more logical level, the sentence means something like *The woman pushed the man and that man was old*. This logical meaning in (17b) can only be extracted by a syntactic analysis, because the linear order of the words is not the same as their logical order in the meaning.

◆  What does the pattern of non-fluent aphasic comprehension deficit, coupled with the speech production data, suggest is going on in non-fluent aphasia?

◆  It seems that people with non-fluent aphasia do not have access to the syntactic mechanisms. These are the processes which deduce the logical relations between different words in a sentence from the form of a sentence. People with non-fluent aphasia are probably guessing at the meaning of sentences just from the individual words involved, and not from access to the syntactic structure of the sentence. For this reason, non-fluent aphasia has also been called *agrammatic aphasia*.

The brain damage in non-fluent aphasia was always thought to be in Broca's area in the left frontal lobe (Figure 2.15). This generalization is probably too simplistic; studies of many aphasic and other neurological patients show that damage to Broca's area does not always produce these symptoms, and that damage to other areas does sometimes produce them. Nonetheless, the most frequent source of these symptoms is damage to Broca's area and the most frequent result of damage to Broca's area is these symptoms.

◆  From the aphasia evidence, what is the function of Broca's area?

◆  Broca's area seems especially involved in the syntactic analysis of a sentence. (It may also have other functions to do with the production of speech, which is why articulation in Broca's patients tends to be distorted.)

In stark contrast to non-fluent aphasia is fluent aphasia. In fluent aphasia, the patient has very obvious comprehension problems. He makes semantic errors with words, such as pointing to his ankle when asked to point to his knee. By contrast, the articulation, intonation and fluency of speech sound normal. For this reason, fluent aphasia was initially thought of as a disorder of comprehension rather than of production. However, linguistic output is far from normal, as illustrated by (18), a fluent aphasic's description of a picture.

(18) Well this is … mother is away here working her work o'here to get her better, but when she's looking, the two boys looking in the other part. One their small tile into her time here. She's working another time because she's getting, too.

◆  Compare and contrast the language of (18) to the language of the non-fluent patient in (15).

◆  Unlike (15), the fluent patient's output is in full sentences, with verbs as well as nouns. There is evidence of grammatical relations; for example, 'is working' is inflected to agree with 'mother'. The non-fluent sample was economically worded but informative, since all the key elements were specified. Here the speech is fluent but the information content is very low. This is because the words selected tend to lack concreteness and specificity of meaning ('working her work' rather than what she is actually doing; 'the other part' rather than the exact place). At other times, it seems that the wrong content words have been selected, and as a consequence the sentence is uninterpretable ('One their small tile into her time here').

◈   From the above, what aspects of language processing would you guess are impaired in fluent aphasia?

◆   Syntax is generally unaffected. There seems to be a specific deficit in semantics. That is, there is trouble hooking the concrete meanings of words, especially nouns, to the objects to which they refer.

This view is reinforced by the fact that fluent aphasia can often be linked to another condition known as **anomia**. Anomia is a deficit in accessing the names of objects. It can take several forms, including the inability to give the name of an object when confronted with a picture of it, or the inability to find a name from a description or definition. One of the most striking discoveries about anomia is that the impairment can be specific to particular categories of things.

There are many patients who have trouble retrieving abstract names, like *supplication*, *pact*, or *culture*, whilst still being able to find relatively concrete ones like *cheese* or *thimble*. This is perhaps not surprising; the abstract meanings tend to be rarer, more complex, and learned later in life, so they might be expected to be the first ones abolished by brain damage. What is striking is that there are also patients in whom the pattern of preservation is the other way around. Some examples of the definitions that this second group of patients volunteer are given in Table 2.1.

**Table 2.1**   Definitions of abstract and concrete words produced by patients with a superiority for abstract words. (Adapted from E.M. Saffran and A. Sholl (1999).)

| Word | Meaning given |
| --- | --- |
| *Patient A.B.* | |
| Supplication | Making a serious request for help |
| Pact | Friendly agreement |
| Cabbage | Eat it |
| Geese | An animal but I've forgotten precisely |
| *Patient S.B.Y.* | |
| Malice | To show bad will against somebody |
| Caution | To be careful how you do something |
| Ink | Food – you put on top of food you are eating – a liquid |
| Cabbage | Use for eating, material – it's usually made from an animal |
| *Patient F.B.* | |
| Society | A large group of people who live in the same manner and share the same principles |
| Culture | A way to learn life's customs; it varies from country to country |
| Duck | A small animal with four legs |
| Thimble | We often say sewing thimble |

These patients clearly have real trouble with the meanings of things that are based on concrete sensory (visual, touch or taste) properties, whereas they have no trouble with meanings that are expressible entirely in terms of other words. There are patients in whom the impairment is even more specific. There are individuals who have trouble finding the names of living things, but are fine with manufactured objects such as tools, and there are other patients with the opposite pattern.

How are we to interpret the loss of concrete word meaning in fluent aphasia and anomia? The best explanation is that there are neuronal circuits somewhere that carry the meanings of individual words by connecting the cells that respond to the phonological shape of that word to other cells which represent its non-linguistic attributes such as smell, colour, taste and so on. These circuits appear to be disrupted in fluent aphasia. In that disorder, the machinery of language is all working but it is not anchored to the concrete, non-linguistic meaning of nouns. These word-meaning circuits clearly have some functional specialization within them, so that the area that represents living things is different from that which represents manufactured objects, which is different again from that which represents abstract concepts.

Damage in fluent aphasia is generally located in the vicinity of Wernicke's area, near the junction of the temporal and parietal lobes. Anomias for various types of nouns are generally a consequence of bilateral temporal lobe damage (Figure 2.16). From this we conclude that the posterior and temporal parts of the language areas are specialized towards the linking of particular words to their concrete meanings. The distinction between living and non-living things probably arises as a consequence of the different modalities we use to identify them. Living things are generally distinguished by their perceptual, particularly visual, properties. A 'thing' being an elephant is related to the way it looks. The circuits associated with anomias for living things are down in the temporal lobe, adjacent to circuits from the visual system that we know are involved in identifying objects. Non-living things, like tools, are more defined by what we do with them (a saw is for cutting wood). It is likely that the circuits for the meanings of these words are hooked up to motor circuits for performing the related actions.

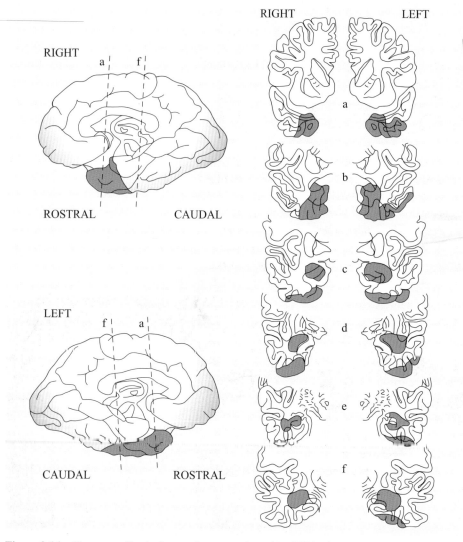

**Figure 2.16**   The areas of brain damage in an anomic patient (F.B.) who was more accurate with abstract than with concrete word meanings. The dark areas are the areas with cortical damage. The series of slices a–f on the right of the figure are coronal sections moving from anterior to posterior.

Anomia, as described here, is a problem with nouns in particular. There are word-finding difficulties associated particularly with verbs, too. They are more particularly associated with frontal lobe damage and non-fluent aphasia. This is a satisfying finding. Verbs are much more 'syntactic' words than nouns. They do not have meaning outside of sentences in quite the way a concrete noun can have, and they are intimately tied up with the creation of sentences, the assigning of subject and object roles and so on. Thus this finding generally supports the view outlined here that sentence processing has a more anterior basis, and individual word meaning has a more posterior one.

## 2.3.4 Specialization within language areas: brain scanning

Is there any evidence from the undamaged brain that the view derived from aphasia is indeed correct? The most useful methodologies here use either PET or functional MRI (fMRI) scanning to establish which parts of the brain are active in particular tasks (Book 3, Section 2.4.1). The difficulty is that a standard linguistic task, such as understanding a sentence's meaning, involves phonology, and syntax, and semantics, and thus is not helpful when trying to tease out which of these subtasks happens in which areas.

Many studies have looked at the pattern of activation produced in the brain by single words. The areas especially active are widespread and somewhat variable, but generally include the auditory cortex on both sides, other parts of the left temporal lobe, and Wernicke's area. A study by Karin Stromswold from the Massachusetts Institute of Technology aimed to identify the areas specialized for the processing of syntax (Stromswold *et al.*, 1996). Her team set up two different conditions of sentence processing. In one condition the participants heard sentences like *The child spilled the juice that stained the rug*, whereas in the other they heard sentences like *The juice that the child spilled stained the rug*. Both of these contain the same words. The first is syntactically quite simple because the order of the nouns in the sentence mirrors their logical relations (child spilled juice, juice stained rug). The second is more complex as the order of its elements does not reflect the logical relations. The areas of the brain specialized for syntax should be more active in the second condition than the first.

The most significant difference between the first and second conditions was indeed that Broca's area was much more active in the second (Figure 2.17). This finding confirms that of several other studies. Thus the view from aphasia seems confirmed; the anterior language areas are specialized for syntax (and verbs and sentence construction), whereas the posterior and temporal ones are more specialized for individual word meanings (and nouns and concreteness). This is doubtless a simplification. There is evidence of significant variability between individuals, and the distinction between areas and subtasks is not watertight. Moreover, we usually do all the subparts of linguistic processing interactively and simultaneously, so something that affects any one part will probably affect them all to a greater or lesser extent. Nonetheless, research in this area is allowing us to understand the anatomy of the language faculty in greater and greater detail.

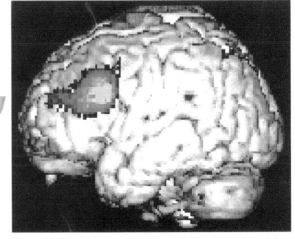

**Figure 2.17** The area of greatest additional brain activity in a series of syntactic as opposed to non-syntactic language tasks imaged using PET scanning. Note that this area corresponds to Broca's area.

## 2.3.5  Electrophysiological studies of language processing

Brain imaging and aphasic studies helped us localize the subparts of language processing within the brain. However, they have shed little light on how processing unfolds in real time. This is because contemporary brain imaging is quite poor at showing changes in activity through time in fine detail, so it is hard to pick up something that may be happening slightly before something else.

In Section 2.2, we identified several tasks that the language processor has to perform – phonological analysis, syntactic analysis, retrieval of word meaning, and so on. We stressed that you cannot always complete one without reference to the others. For example, a signal which is phonologically ambiguous might be resolved by the context, or the rest of the sentence might determine which of several possible meanings should be given to a particular word. But which happens first? Do they all take place in parallel? Do they each work independently, or is there cross-talk between them?

There is a general controversy within linguistics about just how much the different processing components interact. In one school of thought, for example, the identification of phonemes and word boundaries goes on autonomously, without access to the likely meanings of words or the context. This is a *modular* model, with processing going on in separate watertight subsystems. The alternative would be an *interactive* approach. In an interactive model, phoneme recognition and segmentation processes would already be influenced by information about what meanings are likely to be conveyed in the context. Even the modular model admits there must be some interaction between different processes. For example, in (7) (in Section 2.2.3), we rejected the second segmentation (7b) on the basis not of its phonological implausibility but because it doesn't mean anything. The difference between the two models lies in where they see the interaction happening. In an interactive account, considerations of meaning enter into the very process of identifying and segmenting the words, blocking (7b) and causing the processor to output (7a).

(7)  (a)  [my] [dads] [tu] [tor]

(b)  [mide] [ad] [stewt] [er]

In a modular account, phonological processing uses acoustic information only. It then outputs to the semantic and syntactic processors 'here are two possible segmentations of this signal' (i.e. 7a and 7b). The semantic and syntactic processors then accept one and suppress the other.

Rather similar issues arise with ambiguous words, as in (19).

(19) (a)  The robber walked into the bank.

(b)  The canoe crashed into the bank.

It has long been known that if the word *bank* is flashed onto a screen, then for quite a long time afterwards, all the meanings associated with banks are primed in a person's brain. The classic way of testing this is what is called a **lexical decision task**. The participant is shown a string of letters and has to decide if they make up a word. The time it takes him to do this is recorded. People who have earlier seen the word *bank* on a screen are subsequently much quicker to decide that *money* is a word. They are also quicker to decide that *river* is a word than those who have not seen the word *bank* earlier. However, they are no quicker to decide that *giraffe* is a word. Thus, the word *bank* partially activates the whole realm of meanings related to it, such that you are then quicker to recognize other elements of that realm when you encounter them. The question, then, is whether in (19a), only the *money house* meaning is ever accessed for *bank*, or whether the *river* meaning is also accessed. If the former is the case, it would be evidence for an interactive account; elements of the context affect the processing of *bank* to the extent that the *river* meaning is never accessed. If the latter is the case, it would be evidence for a modular account; *bank* primes *river*, automatically, and without regard for the context.

Interestingly, what happens in this case is that *river* is primed for just a few seconds after presentation of (19a), but the priming then fades away rapidly. By contrast, *money* is primed immediately after presentation, and then stays primed. Sentence (19b) produces the opposite effect. This can be taken as evidence for a modular account; all the possible meanings of *bank* are primed, automatically, by the processing of *bank*. It is only subsequently that the integration of the word *bank* into the sentence context suppresses the other meanings.

This stage-like model is supported by direct recording of brain activity whilst linguistic processing is going on. This recording is done by placing electrodes over the scalp, and they pick up small changes in electrical activity caused by changes in neuronal activity in the brain. The participant is then given an experimental and a control task to do. Differences between the patterns of electrical activity in the control and the experimental task can then be investigated. This technique is known as event-related potential (ERP) recording (see Book 3, Section 2.4.1). It lacks the precision of localization that is provided by brain imaging but it has the advantage of very fine temporal resolution, and thus is informative about the time course of the brain's response to a stimulus.

ERPs are hard to interpret without well-designed experiments. The classic ERP paradigm for studying language is to construct sentences that are for some reason hard to process, and compare the ERP trace of these sentences to that of ordinary ones (Friederici, 2002). For example, sentences where one word is semantically out of context and thus for which it is hard to find a meaning, produce a deviation in the activity trace across the middle of the brain about 400 milliseconds after the deviant word (Figure 2.18). This deviation is known as the N400. It is fairly consistent in two respects; it begins at around 400 milliseconds after the key word, and it is only provoked by *semantic* anomalies; that is sentences which are grammatically correct but weird in meaning.

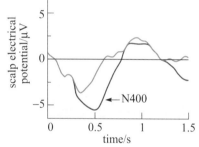

**Figure 2.18**  Event-related potential trace for *The shirt was ironed* (blue line) versus *The thunderstorm was ironed* (red line). The key word is *ironed*, and the deviation is called the N400.

◈    In Figure 2.18, which sentence is semantically normal, and which is semantically anomalous?

◆    *The shirt was ironed* is semantically normal. *The thunderstorm was ironed* is semantically anomalous. We do not expect thunderstorms to be ironed – indeed it is hard to see what this could mean. (*The thunderstorm was ironed* produces an N400 deviation.)

Sentences where the difficulty is syntactic provoke two kinds of deviation. An ungrammatical sentence, like *The shirt was on ironed* produces a deviation in activity over the left frontal lobe, often within a couple of hundred milliseconds of the word *ironed* (Figure 2.19). This deviation is called the LAN (left anterior negativity).

◈    Why do you think the LAN is observed specifically over the left frontal lobe?

◆    This is the site of Broca's area, which we believe to have important syntactic functions.

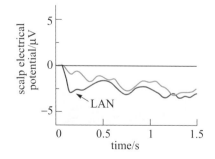

**Figure 2.19**  Anterior event-related potential trace for *The shirt was ironed* (blue line) versus *The shirt was on ironed* (red line). The key word is *ironed*, and the deviation is called the LAN.

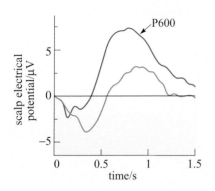

**Figure 2.20**   Posterior event-related potential trace for *The shirt was ironed* (blue line) versus *The shirt was on ironed* (red line). The key word is *ironed*, and the deviation is called the P600.

A second deviation is also produced by syntactic complexities, somewhat later and more posterior in the brain. This deviation is called the P600, and typically peaks around 600 milliseconds after the key word (Figure 2.20). The P600 is produced by grammatical violations, and also by sentences that are syntactically tricky or ambiguous. Sentences like *The shirt was on ironed* produce a LAN *and* a P600. Other sentences, like *The horse raced past the barn fell* produce a P600 but no LAN.

◆   What do you think the cause of the P600 might be, and how does this differ from the LAN?

◆   Both the P600 and the LAN follow syntactic anomalies. The LAN is triggered by gross violations of syntax which are immediately obvious. In *The shirt was on ironed* there is no way that the string of words can ever be grammatical, since *on* must be followed with a noun phrase, and *ironed* is a verb. *The horse raced past the barn fell* is not ungrammatical. There is no violation and therefore the LAN is not produced. However, it is a difficult sentence to integrate conceptually; one tends to start off down one track and then have to switch interpretations. The P600 reflects this extra cognitive work; the search for an appropriate conceptual representation of the sentence.

Note that the LAN happens more quickly than the response to the semantics of the words (the N400), and that the P600 occurs after the initial syntactic and semantic responses have occurred. This has been taken as evidence for a three-stage account of sentence processing. First, there is an initial syntactic analysis of the sentence, mainly in or around Broca's area. This happens within a couple of hundred milliseconds, and produces the LAN. It probably identifies the key lexical elements, whose individual meanings must then be processed.

Semantic processing of the key components of the sentence then follows. This happens further back in the brain, and produces the N400. Finally, the structure and meaning of the sentence is established by integrating semantic and syntactic information. This is straightforward for simple sentences, but where the words or structure are ambiguous, it may mean revising the initial syntactic analysis, or suppressing alternative meanings. This is probably the stage at which the unwanted senses of *bank* are suppressed in (19). It is the stage at which you decide whether sentences like *They are hunting dogs* is a description of dogs or a description of what the hunters are doing. The extra work that may be required at this stage is reflected in the P600 which is produced by complex and ambiguous sentences.

Neat evidence for this three-stage model comes from the response to doubly anomalous sentences, like (20).

(20) The thunderstorm was in ironed.

◆   What ERP responses might you expect that (20) would produce?

◆   You would expect a LAN, because the sentence is grossly ungrammatical. You would also expect an N400, because of the semantic anomaly of *thunderstorm ... ironed*.

What is observed in response to (20) is in fact a LAN, but no N400. This means that the sentence gets blocked at the initial syntactic analysis stage, and is not 'passed on' to the semantic system for meaning analysis.

Such evidence supports a stage-like and somewhat modular account of sentence processing. First the phonology makes available a representation of the sentence. Then an initial syntactic analysis (in the left frontal lobe) assigns a basic structure to the sentence, and then passes on the key words for processing the meaning. The semantic system then makes available the possible meanings. This all happens within half a second. Finally, there is a conceptual integration of syntax and semantics, starting at about 600 milliseconds. Note that the sentence itself must be kept available in a buffer or short-term memory all this time, in case the parsing proves wrong and a re-analysis is necessary.

## Summary of Section 2.3

Sound waves received by the ear are turned into neural activity by a complex mechanism involving the eardrum, the bones in the middle ear, and the hair cells within the cochlea. The auditory nerve carries the signal from the ears to the brainstem, from where it passes via the thalamus to the auditory areas of the cerebral cortex. In the cortex, speech sounds are extracted from the incoming signal. There are neural circuits in the auditory cortex that are specialized for speech and language as opposed to other types of sound.

Production and perception of speech takes place predominantly in one hemisphere of the brain, usually the left. Several areas within the left hemisphere are involved. Broca's area, in the frontal lobe, seems to be crucial for syntactic operations in both production and perception of speech. Wernicke's area, in the temporal lobe, seems to be crucial for accessing the concrete meanings of words. The evidence for the distinction in function between posterior and anterior language areas comes from the study of aphasia, that is, problems with language resulting from brain injury, as well as brain scanning.

Evidence from electrophysiological recording suggests that decoding a sentence involves several stages. First, there is an initial syntactic analysis of the structure of the sentence. Then the meanings of the individual words are accessed. Finally, the meanings of the individual words and the structure of the sentence are integrated to produce a coherent overall meaning. This all happens within one second of the final word being uttered.

## 2.4  Conclusions

### Activity 2.3

Read back over Section 2.3. Make two columns on a piece of paper, one headed 'finding', and one headed 'evidence'. Make a list of key findings we have established about the processing of language in the brain. For example, your first finding might be 'Language localized to the left', and the evidence might be 'aphasia, brain scanning', and so on. The findings might be of two sorts the evidence of locations (i.e. where things happen), and the evidence of processes (i.e. the sequence in which they happen).

The first half of this chapter showed just how complex human language is; in the second half, we have established some preliminary findings about how the brain masters it. We clearly have a lot of finely structured special neural machinery to pull off this complex task. We have hardly touched on where this machinery comes from (though see Box 2.2 overleaf). Scientists have only just scratched the surface of language. It has been hard to identify the relevant processes in the brain because the

## Box 2.2    The language instinct?

We have seen in this chapter that there is a great deal of apparently specialized neural machinery for language, from language-specific areas in the auditory cortex, to Broca's area and its role in syntax. Where does this specialized machinery come from? Is it the effect of frequent practice from an early age that makes these structures become dedicated to language?

An influential school of thought in linguistics argues that the capacity for language is innate. Of course, this does not mean that English, German or Swahili is encoded genetically. Rather, the acquisition of a language is a genetically initiated and genetically guided process. It certainly seems like there is something in this view. The acquisition of language unfolds in a similar pattern across different cultures. It does not seem to matter whether parents attempt to explicitly teach their children or not; as long as there is some linguistic input around, children will acquire a language. At peak rate, children acquire something like one new word per hour. The linguist Noam Chomsky has argued for decades that this process is much more like growth in stature than learning to play the piano; as long as there is adequate nutrition, it will just happen, because it is programmed to do so.

The main argument for Chomsky's position has always been logical rather than empirical. The child has to infer a grammar, quickly, on the basis of the sentences flying around above his head. These sentences contain positive examples of what a grammatical sentence is, but no negative evidence. Parents do not say *the cat sitting is mat the on* followed by a small electric shock to condition children away from ungrammatical sentences. Rather, the child has to figure out the grammar with no examples of what sort of things it does *not* allow. Chomsky has argued that it would be impossible to do this without fairly strong innate principles to guide the process (for example, the innate knowledge that the

language will contain nouns and verbs, subjects and objects, put constraints on what sequences of sounds are possible, etc.). The data alone are not enough to allow the acquisition of language; you need some guiding principles already laid down.

The exact content of this 'start-up pack' is very hard to determine. So too is the adequacy of Chomsky's argument, which is called the **argument from the poverty of the stimulus**. We simply do not know nearly enough about the overall architecture of cognition, or the mental representation of language, to know how much needs to be specified beforehand and how much will just emerge in interaction with the environment and other cognitive systems. However, it does seem fairly clear that language is a species-specific behaviour, and thus part of our biology and evolution rather than our cultural history.

Interesting light has been shed recently on the innateness debate by the study of a genetic disorder called **specific language impairment (SLI)**. Affected individuals have rather specific problems with grammar, like getting the inflection right in *The man wants to go* versus *The man want to go*. In some families, the disorder is controlled by a single gene, called FOXP2 (Lai *et al.*, 2001), and all the affected individuals in these families carry a particular allele that is not present in other families. Intriguingly, FOXP2 is present in other primates but the gene there differs from that in humans. Is FOXP2 one of the genes encoding Chomsky's innate linguistic principles?

The story seems unlikely to be a simple one. It has recently been shown that people affected by SLI have a wide range of other difficulties, from IQ scores to complex facial movements. If the gene involved is a gene for grammar, it is also a gene involved in other things too.

precise identification of neural activity in space and time is something we have only just started being able to do. Moreover, just to achieve a correct characterization of the behaviour whose neural bases we are seeking took a long time.

There are still many unanswered questions. For example, the binding problem is the question of how the meaning *green* gets stuck to the meaning *dog*, and not something else, in (14c). Our best guess about how this happens neurally is as follows. There is a localized circuit which encodes the meaning of *green*, and this starts firing in response to a sentence with the word *green* in it. There is another circuit for *dog*, which fires when the word *dog* is present. If the syntax says that these two meanings are bound together in the particular sentence, then their firing becomes synchronous. If they are in the same sentence but not bound together, they both fire, but asynchronously.

Now this account may very well be correct, but it poses an obvious problem. How then do we process the meaning of (21)?

(21) The green cat is beside the blue cat, not the green dog.

The *green* circuit would have to be synchronous with both *cat* and *dog*. The *cat* circuit would have to be synchronous with both *green* and *blue*. Yet the meaning of the sentence is not a cat that is both green and blue. The bindings are kept separate. We have no real idea how this is done. This is the wonderful thing about human language. Like the pattern of an ice crystal, the closer you probe it, the more complexities of structure there are. The adventure is only just beginning …

## Learning outcomes for Chapter 2

After studying this chapter, you should be able to:

2.1 Recognize definitions and applications of each of the terms printed in **bold** in the text.

2.2 Understand and apply basic grammatical terminology.

2.3 Describe briefly the different types of sounds used in speech in both acoustic and articulatory terms.

2.4 Outline the key features of human language as compared to the vocalizations of other species.

2.5 Describe the complex psychological processes involved in decoding even simple sentences of spoken language.

2.6 Describe briefly how auditory information is converted into brain activity by the human ear.

2.7 Describe different types of language impairment caused by brain damage, and relate these to the way language is processed in the intact brain.

2.8 Explain the different sources of evidence used by researchers in trying to understand how language is processed in the brain.

2.9 Describe the probable stages in the decoding of a sentence of spoken language in the cortex of the brain.

## Questions for Chapter 2

### Question 2.1    *(Learning outcomes 2.1 and 2.2)*

Define each of the following: grammar, phonology, syntax, semantics, noun, verb, subject, object.

### Question 2.2    *(Learning outcome 2.3)*

For each of the following words, identify the vowels and the consonants which are produced when the word is spoken. Bear in mind that English spelling doesn't bear a close relationship to the way the language is spoken today. The first example is done for you. Note: The precise spelling you use is unimportant for present purposes – just try to spell it like it actually sounds. The point of the question is to identify phonological units. (These will be slightly different depending on which dialect of English you have.)

nightmare    nai    t    m    ee
               V    C    C    V

psychology

subtle

meaning

monkey

yearning

### Question 2.3    *(Learning outcome 2.4)*

Use the information you noted down as part of Activity 2.1, to fill in the following table comparing the vocal communication systems of vervet monkeys with human language, using the options on the right:

|  | Vervet calls | Human language |  |
|---|---|---|---|
| Number of meanings |  |  | large, small |
| Generativity |  |  | present, absent |
| Elements can be combined |  |  | yes, no |
| Meaning depends on context |  |  | yes, no |
| Syntax |  |  | present, absent |
| Noun/verb distinction |  |  | present, absent |
| Acoustic distinctiveness of different signals |  |  | great, small |

## Question 2.4   *(Learning outcome 2.5)*

Explain in your own terms why each of the following sentences might be difficult for people to process when heard aloud:

(a) The dog it was that the cat chased.

(b) The boy the man the woman knew liked went away.

(c) The horse raced past the barn fell.

## Question 2.5   *(Learning outcome 2.6)*

How do hair cells detect sound, and how is this signal converted into neural activity?

## Question 2.6   *(Learning outcome 2.7)*

What are the symptoms of fluent aphasia? How do these differ from those of non-fluent aphasia?

## Question 2.7   *(Learning outcome 2.8)*

How do we know that the capacity for language is localized predominantly in the left hemisphere?

## Question 2.8   *(Learning outcome 2.9)*

What are the three stages of sentence processing that have been identified by studies using ERPs? What is the name of the ERP component associated with each stage?

### Question 1.1

The figure illustrating your performance shows that your memory for nonsense syllables decays to almost zero in about 20 seconds. This is because only your working memory was engaged in this task and memories stored in working memory typically decay within seconds. You did notice that when you actively rehearsed the syllable, your ability to remember it was improved. This improvement arises because you have now engaged your short-term memory.

### Question 1.2

The hippocampus plays a key role in the process of consolidation of memory in mammals, especially declarative memories. However, motor skill learning (for which procedural memories are formed) does not necessarily utilize the hippocampus. Likewise, H.M. could learn certain motor skills despite the fact that his declarative memory was severely impaired by the surgical removal of his medial temporal lobe including the hippocampus.

### Question 1.3

The woman has a normal memory for events in the distant past and a normal memory for events occurring a minute or so before recall; otherwise conversation would have been impossible. The problem was either that she could not consolidate new memories, or that events recently consolidated were inaccessible (hence the failure to recall the near past).

### Question 1.4

The correct answer is (D). Inhibition of protein synthesis means that new proteins are not made. Potassium permeability (A), neurotransmission (B), frequency of action potentials (C), and short-term memory (E) do not require new protein synthesis, and so would be unaffected by the protein synthesis inhibitor. (F) is nonsense, since there is not a stable molecule code for memory.

### Question 1.5

A   False – release of neurotransmitter from the presynaptic terminal is in itself not sufficient to modify the synapse. For Hebbian learning to occur, both the presynaptic cell and the postsynaptic cell need to be active at the same time – though a threshold level of postsynaptic depolarization must be achieved.

B   False – NMDA receptors are involved in both the induction of LTP and learning. Pharmacological blockade of NMDA receptors prevents spatial learning in the Morris water maze.

C   True – NMDA receptors are voltage-dependent. This property arises because at resting membrane potential, the NMDA receptor channel is blocked by extracellular magnesium ions. In order for the NMDA receptor to contribute to the synaptic potential, the postsynaptic membrane must first be depolarized to repel the magnesium ions from the NMDA channel.

D   True – the Hebbian nature is conferred by the absolute requirement for (i) neurotransmitter to be present and (ii) the removal of the magnesium block of the NMDA channel by strong postsynaptic depolarization (coincidence detector).

E   False – the voltage-dependency of the NMDA receptor is attributable to extracellular magnesium ions. It is the entry of calcium into the postsynaptic cell, through the NMDA receptor that triggers the biochemical cascade that gives rise to LTP, etc.

F   False – long-term depression can also be induced in an activity-dependent manner at mammalian synapses.

## Question 2.1

Grammar: The set of unconscious rules or principles that the speaker of a human language brings to bear when producing or understanding speech.

Phonology: The part of grammar dealing with permissible combinations of sounds into words.

Syntax: The part of grammar concerned with the rules for legitimately combining words into sentences.

Semantics: The part of grammar dealing with the meanings of words and sentences.

Noun: A class of word that can take the role of the subject of a sentence. A noun usually denotes an object or person, though this is not always the case.

Verb: A class of word that usually requires the presence of at least one noun to form a grammatical sentence. Verbs usually denote actions or processes.

Subject: The primary grammatical role a noun may play in a sentence. The role of the subject may be as the doer or initiator of an action, or bearer of a quality.

Object: Any noun in a sentence other than the subject. It often denotes the target or recipient of an action.

## Question 2.2

These answers are for the author's own Southern England dialect of English.

| psychology | s | ai | k | o | l | o | dg | ee |
|---|---|---|---|---|---|---|---|---|
| | C | V | C | V | C | V | C | V |
| subtle | s | u | t | u[1] | l | | | |
| | C | V | C | V | C | | | |
| meaning | m | ee | n | i | ng[2] | | | |
| | C | V | C | V | C | | | |
| monkey | m | u | n | k | ee | | | |
| or | m | u | ng | k | ee | | | |
| | C | V | C | V | C | | | |
| yearning | y | e[3] | n | i | ng[2] | | | |
| | C | V | C | V | C | | | |

[1] This is a sound, very common in English, called schwa, which has no consistent representation in our spelling.

[2] This is pronounced as one sound.

[3] This is a difficult vowel to capture using the ordinary alphabet, but it is a single sound.

Did you find yourself tempted to put in letters because they are there in the spelling, only to find on careful thought that they are not in the spoken form at all?

## Question 2.3

|  | Vervet calls | Human language |
| --- | --- | --- |
| Number of meanings | small | large |
| Generativity | absent | present |
| Elements can be combined | no | yes |
| Meaning depends on context | no | yes |
| Syntax | absent | present |
| Noun/verb distinction | absent | present |
| Acoustic distinctiveness of different signals | great | small |

## Question 2.4

(a) The first noun you come to is not actually the subject of the sentence. The subject is the cat, and the object is the dog, but they appear in the opposite order.

(b) This is what is known as a centre-embedded sentence. This means that the 'went away' actually binds with 'the boy', but there is other material embedded in the middle which makes this difficult to see.

(c) This is what is called a 'garden-path' sentence. As you read it, you at first think it means that the horse raced past the barn. It actually can only mean that 'the horse [which was] raced past the barn fell' but this only becomes clear when you reach 'the fell'. This means you have to revise your sketch of what the structure of the sentence is. It is normal to have to read it a few times before seeing that it was not the barn that fell, and the horse did not race, but was raced by someone else.

## Question 2.5

Hair cells have tiny hairs (cilia) on them. Vibrations from the air are transmitted into the cochlea, where they cause the hairs to move. Within the cell, movements of the cilia are converted into electrical impulses. Hair cells have synapses with neurons of the auditory nerve, and so their electrical changes become action potentials which are transmitted to the brain.

## Question 2.6

In fluent aphasia, the sentences are complete and the grammatical relations are often normal. However, the information content is very low. The words chosen are either generalized or inappropriate in meaning. By contrast, in non-fluent aphasia, the right content words are selected but they are not strung together into full sentences.

## Question 2.7

There are several lines of evidence:

1   Brain damage to the left hemisphere causes aphasia more often than does damage to the right hemisphere.

2    Injection of a rapid acting anaesthetic into the left carotid artery (which suppresses the left cerebral hemisphere) tends to cause loss of speech, whereas injection into the right carotid does so less often. A similar procedure can be done with electrical stimulation of the cortex.

3    'Split-brain' patients whose corpus callosum has been severed tend to be able to talk about the stimuli on the right side of their visual field or in their right hand. The right side is connected to the left hemisphere of the brain.

4    Brain imaging techniques such as PET scanning.

## Question 2.8

Phonology makes available a basic representation of the sentence.

1    An initial syntactic analysis assigns a basic structure to the sentence (starting within 200 ms). This stage is called LAN.

2    The meaning of key words is processed (normally within 400 ms). This stage is known as N400.

3    Syntax and semantics are integrated (normally within 600 ms). If they do not fit together, the sentence, which is still stored in short-term memory, is re-analysed. This stage is known as P600.

# Chapter 1

## References

Bliss, T. V. P. and Lømo, T. (1973) Long-lasting potentiation of synaptic transmission in the dentate area of the anaesthetized rabbit following stimulation of the perforant path, *Journal of Physiology*, **232**, pp. 331–56.

Luria, A. R. (1987) *The Mind of a Mnemonist,* in Squire, L. R. (1987) *Memory and Brain*, Oxford University Press, Oxford.

Morris, R. G. M. (1984) Development of a water-maze procedure for studying spatial learning in the rat, *Journal of Neuroscience Methods*, **11**, pp. 47–60.

Rogan, M. T., Stäubli, U. V. and LeDoux, J. E. (1997) Fear conditioning induces associative long-term potentiation in the amygdala, *Nature*, **390**, pp. 604–7.

## Further reading

Toates, F. (2001) *Biological Psychology: An Integrative Approach*, Prentice Hall, Harlow.

Kandel, E. R., Schwartz, J. H. and Jessell, T. M. (2000) *Principles of Neural Science*, 4th edn, McGraw-Hill, New York.

Dudai, Y. (1989) *The Neurobiology of Memory: Concepts, Findings, Trends*, Oxford University Press, Oxford.

# Chapter 2

## References

Berndt, R. S., Mitchum, C. C. and Wayland, S. (1997) Patterns of sentence comprehension in aphasia: A consideration of three hypotheses, *Brain and Language*, **60**, pp. 197–221.

Friederici, A. D. (2002) Towards a neural basis of auditory sentence processing, *Trends in Cognitive Sciences*, **6**, pp. 78–84.

Lai, C. S. L., Fisher, S. E., Hurst, J. A., Vargha-Khadem, F. and Monaco, A. P. (2001) A forkhead-domain gene is mutated in a severe speech and language disorder, *Nature*, **413**, pp. 519–23.

Moore, D. R. (2000) Auditory neuroscience: Is speech special? *Current Biology*, **10**, R362–R364.

Saffran, E. M. and Sholl, A. (1999) Clues to the functional and neural architecture of word meaning, in C. M. Brown and P. Hagoort (eds) *The Neurocognition of Language*, Oxford University Press, Oxford, pp. 241–72.

Seyfarth, R. M., Cheney, D. L. and Marler, P. (1980) Vervet monkey alarm calls: Semantic communication in a free-ranging primate, *Animal Behaviour*, **28**, pp. 1070–94.

Stromswold, K., Caplan, D., Alpert, N. and Rauch, S. (1996) Localization of syntactic comprehension by positron emission tomography, *Brain and Language*, **52**, pp. 452–73.

## Further reading

The following book gives a good (introductory) account of Chomsky's ideas on the origin of language:

Pinker, S. (1994) *The Language Instinct*, Penguin, London.

A more advanced book on the nature of language:

Jackendoff, R. (2003) *Foundations of Language: Brain, Meaning, Grammar, Evolution*, Oxford University Press, Oxford.

On hearing and speech:

Denes, P. B. and Pinson, E. N. (1993) *The Speech Chain: The Physics and Biology of Spoken Language*, 2nd edn, W.H. Freeman, New York.

On the processing of language and speech in the brain:

Brown, C. M. and Hagoort, P. (eds) (2002) *The Neurocognition of Language*, Oxford University Press, Oxford.

The following book is a very good introduction to sound, spectral analysis and speech:

Rosen, S. and Howel, P. (1991) *Signals and Systems for Speech and Hearing*, Academic Press, London.

# ACKNOWLEDGEMENTS

Grateful acknowledgement is made to the following sources for permission to reproduce material within this product.

*Cover*

*Persistence of Memory* by Salvador Dali (Scala Picture Library);

*Figures*

*Figure 1.6* Blakemore, C. (1997) *Mechanics in the Mind*, Cambridge University Press; *Figure 1.7* Farah, M. (1990) *Visual Agnosia*, The MIT Press; *Figures 1.8, 1.15 and 1.28* Kandel, E. R., Schwartz, J. H. and Jessell, T. M. (eds) (2000) *Principles of Neural Science*, 4th edn, McGraw-Hill. Copyright © 2000 by The McGraw-Hill Companies, Inc. All rights reserved; *Figure 1.9* Copyright © Nicky Clayton; *Figure 1.11* Alfred Pasieka/Science Photo Library *Figure 1.12* Courtesy of The Babraham Institute; *Figures 1.13a, 1.13b and 1.20* Chapman, P. F. *et al.* (1999) 'Impaired synaptic plasticity and learning in aged amyloid precursor protein transgenic mice', *Nature Neuroscience*, Vol. 2, No. 3, March 1999, © Nature America Inc; *Figures 1.14a, 1.14b, 1.14c and 1.14d* Kandel, E. R., Schwartz, J. H. and Jessell, T. M. (eds) (2000) *Essentials of Neural Science and Behavior*, McGraw-Hill. Copyright © 2000 by The McGraw-Hill Companies, Inc. All rights reserved; *Figure 1.19* Copyright © Alaa El-Husseini, University of British Columbia; *Figures 1.22a and 1.22b* Reprinted from Progress in *Neurobiology*, Vol. 55, No. 2, 1998, Brown, M. W. and Xiang, J-Z. 'Recognition memory: Neuronal substrates of the judgement of prior occurrence', Page 15. Copyright © 1998 with permission from Elsevier; *Figures 1.22c* Cho, K. *et al.* (2000) 'A new form of long-term depression in the perirhinal cortex' *Nature Neuroscience*, Vol. 3, No. 3, February 2000. Copyright © Nature America Inc; *Figure 1.23* Morris, R. G. *et al.* (1986) 'Selective impairment of learning and blockade of long term potentiation by an N-methyl', *Nature*, Vol. 319, No. 6053, 27 February 1986, Nature Publications; *Figure 1.24* Squire, L. R. and Schlapfer, W. T. (1981) 'Memory and memory disorders: A biological and neurologic perspective' in van Praag, H. M. *et al.*, *Handbook of Biological Psychiatry Part IV* 1981, Marcel Dekker; *Figure 1.26* Rogan, M. T., Staubli, U. V. and LeDoux, J. E. (1997) *Nature*, Vol. 390, pp. 604–7, Nature Publishing Group; *Figure 1.27* Rogan, M. T. (1997) 'Fear conditioning association long-term potentiation in amygdala', *Nature*, Vol. 390, 11 December 1997, Nature Publishers Ltd; *Figure 1.29* Purves, D. *et al.* (2001) *Neuroscience*, Sinauer Associates Inc;

*Figure 2.1* Copyright © Tony Camacho/Science Photo Library; *Figures 2.3, 2.5, 2.6 and 2.9* Courtesy of Daniel Nettle; *Figure 2.7* Holly, R. *et al.* (1997) 'Neurobiology of speech perception', *Annual Review of Neuroscience*, **20**. Copyright © 1997 by Annual Reviews Inc. All rights reserved; *Figure 2.8* Peterson, G. E. and Barney, H. L. (1952) 'Control method used in a study of vowels', *The Journal of the Acoustical Society of America*, Vol. 24, No. 2, March 1952. The Acoustical Society of America. Used by permission of the American Institute of Physics; *Figure 2.11* Copyright © VVG/Science Photo Library; *Figure 2.12* Martini *et al.* (2000, Fig 18–17, p. 483) in Toates, F. (2001) 'The other sensory systems', in *Biological Psychology*, Pearson Education; *Figure 2.16* Sirigu, A. *et al.* (1991) 'The role of sensorimotor experience in object recognition', *Brain*, Part VI, p. 2558, by permission of Oxford University Press; *Figure 2.17* Indefrey, P. *et al.* (1998) 'Specific response of the left inferior frontal sulcus to syntactic processing' (manuscript), by permission of Dr Peter Indefrey; *Figures 2.18, 2.19 and 2.20* Reprinted from *Trends in Cognitive Sciences*, Vol. 6, No. 2, Friederici, A. D., 'Towards a neural basis of auditory sentence processing', p. 81, Copyright © 2002, with permission from Elsevier.

Every effort has been made to contact copyright holders. If any have been inadvertently overlooked the publishers will be pleased to make the necessary arrangements at the first opportunity.

# INDEX

Glossary terms are in bold. Italics indicate items mainly, or wholly, in a figure or table.

## A

abstract words, 71–2

accidents, causing amnesia, 3

acoustic energy, 54–5, 57

action potential,
    in synapses, 12–13, *14*
    for working memory, 42

adjectives, 51

adverbs, 51

afferent pathway, stimulation, 30, *31, 33*

agnosia, 19, *20*

agrammatic aphasia, 70

Alzheimer's disease, 24, *25,* 26
    synaptic plasticity, 33, *34*

ambiguous words, 74, 76

American one cent coin, memory of, 44, *45*

amnesia,
    effect of cycloheximide, 39, *40*
    patient H.M., 18–19
    retrograde, 3, 40
    *see also* forgetfulness

AMPA receptors, 34–6

amygdala, conditioning response, *41*

amyloid plaques, 24, *25,* 26

amyloid precursor protein (APP), 25–6

animals, *see* mammals

**anomia, 71**–3

**aphasia, 67,** 68–73

*Aphelocoma californica* (scrub jay), 21–2

*Aplysia* (sea slug), 27–9

apperceptive agnosia, 19, *20*

arachidonic acid, 36

**argument from the poverty of the stimulus, 78**

assimilation, 58

associative agnosia, 19, *20*

associative conditioning, 7

associative long-term potentiation (LTP), *32*

auditory cortex, *65, 66*

**auditory nerve, 64,** 65

**auditory ossicles, 64**–5

## B

**basilar membrane, 64**–5

behaviourists, 9

bell experiment, classical conditioning, 6, 7, 13–15, 32

**binding problem, 62**–3, 79

birds,
    scrub jay, 21–2
    spatial learning, 21–4

blinking, reflex response, 6–7, 8, 14

brain,
    in Alzheimer's disease, 24, *25*
    frontal lobe, 67, *68*
    language areas, 73
    language processing, 67–8
    speech perception, 64–7
    synapse linkages, 12–13
    *see also* cortex

brain damage, *see* Alzheimer's disease; aphasia

brain imaging studies, 67–8

brain scanning, 73

Broca's aphasia, 68–70

Broca's area, 67–8, 73, 76

## C

CA1 region of hippocampus, *21, 30*

CA3 region of hippocampus, *21, 30*

calcium ions, 35, 36

calls, animal, 49, 52, *55,* 60

**categorical perception, 58**

*Ceropithecus aethiops* (vervet monkey), 49, 52, *55,* 60

chemotherapy, 17

Chomsky, Noam, 78

classical conditioning, 5–7
    Hebbian learning, 12–13
    Hebbian synapses, 13–15
    long-term potentiation, 31–2
    re-examined, 10–11

clauses, 63

**co-articulation, 58,** *59*

**cochlea, 64**–5

cognitive map, 10, 24

comprehension, in anaphasia, 69–72

concrete words, 71–2

**conditional response, 6, 7,** 8, 11

**conditional stimulus, 6, 7,** 8, 11

conditioning, 10–11
    nomenclature of, 7–8
    *see also* classical conditioning; instrumental conditioning

conditioning tetanus, 30, *31,* 32

conjunctions, 51

consolidation of memory, 20, 39

**consonants, 56**–7, 58

cooperativity, 32

cortex,
    auditory, *65,* 66
    prefrontal, 42
    primary auditory, *65,* 66
    role in memory, 19
    temporal, *37*

cortical glutamatergic synapses, 37

cortical lesions, effect on memory, 19–20

cycloheximide, 39, *40*

## D

dancing bears, 11

**declarative memory, 4**–5
    effect of cortical lesions, 19–20
    patient H.M., 18–19
    in spatial learning, 23

dendrate gyrus, *21, 26, 30*

depolarization, postsynaptic, 32–3, *35*

dialects, 58

diphthongs, *55,* 56

dogs,
    classical conditioning, 5–7
    learning tricks, 8
    paw lifting, 15–16

**duality of patterning, 53**–4

# E

eagle, vervet monkey call, 49, 52, *55*, 60

ears, speech perception, 64–5

electrophysiological studies, language processing, 74–7

encoding of memory, 20

entorhinal cortex, *21, 30, 37*

epilepsy, 67, 68

**episodic memory**, **4**–5

event-related potential (ERP) recording, 75–6

eye movements, and working memory, 42–3

# F

fear, conditioning response, *40, 41*

fluent aphasia, 68, 70–3

food,
 classical conditioning, 6, 7, 13–15, 32
 Garcia effect, 17
 salivation response, 5–6

food caches, 22

forgetfulness, *3*, 44–5
 *see also* amnesia

**formant frequencies**, **54**–5, 56

FOXP2 gene, 78

frequency of sound, 54–6

frontal lobe, 67, *68*, 70, 75

**fundamental frequency**, **54**–5

# G

Garcia effect, 17

**generative**, **53**

**generativity**, **52**

genetic mutation, in Alzheimer's disease, 25–6, 33, *34*

gill-withdrawal response, 27–8

glutamate receptors, 34, *35*

**grammar**, **50**–1

**grammatical**, **50**–1

# H

habituation, 27–8, 29

**hair cells**, **64**–5

**harmonic**, **54**

Hebb, Donald, 12, 13

Hebbian learning, 12–13
 instrumental conditioning, 15–17

Hebbian synapses,
 classical conditioning, 13–15

hippocampus, 30–4
 mechanics of, 34–8

hemispheres of the brain, 67

hippocampus, *21, 30*
 in Alzheimer's disease, 24, *25*, 26

Hebbian synapses, 30–4
 role in memory, 19, 21–4

H.M., memory loss, 18–19

hunger, rat conditioning, 9–10, 15, 16

Huntington's disease, 33

hyperphosphorylation, *25*, 26

# I

innateness of language, 78

instrumental conditioning, 8, 9, 10
 Hebbian learning, 15–17

interactive model of language processing, 74–5

International Phonetic Alphabet (IPA), *56*

intransitive verbs, 51–2

# K

**kinases**, **36**

# L

language, 49–52
 acquisition, 78
 generativity and patterning, 52–4
 meanings, 60–2
 phonology, 50, 54–60
 syntax, 62–4
 *see also* linguistics; syntax

language processing,
 in the brain, 67–8
 electrophysiological studies, 74–7

lateralization in the brain, 67

learning,
 instrumental conditioning, 15–16
 long-term potentiation (LTP), 38–42
 neuron interconnections, 27–9
 synapse activity, 30
 synaptic depression, 37–8
 *see also* Hebbian learning; spatial learning

left anterior negativity (LAN), 75–6

left frontal lobe, 68, 70, 75

left hemisphere of the brain, 67

leopard, vervet monkey call, 49, 52, *55*, 60

lever pressing experiment, 8–9

**lexical decision task**, **74**

linguistics,
 impairments, 67, 68–73
 language acquisition, 78
 processing models, 74
 *see also* language

London taxi drivers, spatial memory, 21

long-term depression (LTD) of synaptic responses, *37*, 38

long-term memory, 2–4
 deterioration of, 44, *45*
 role of hippocampus, 19

**long-term potentiation (LTP)**, **30**–4
 link with learning, 38–42
 trigger and maintenance, 35–6

Luria, A.R., 44

# M

magnesium ions, 34, *35*

mammals,
 instrumental conditioning, 8, *9*
 spatial learning, 21–4
 *see also* dogs; mice; monkeys; rats; sheep

maze experiment, 9–10, 15, 16
 water maze, 22, *23*, 24, 38, *39*

memory,
 long-term, 2–4, 19, 44, *45*
 long-term potentiation (LTP), 38–42
 object recognition, 37
 phenomenal, 44
 short-term, 2–4
 storage and retrieval, 1–2, 20–1
 types of, 4–5
 working, 3–4, 42–5
 *see also* declarative memory; procedural memory

memory loss, *see* amnesia

mental arithmetic, 3–4

mice, Alzheimer's disease, 26

modular account, 74–5

monkeys,
 alarm calls, 49, 52, *55*, 60
 working memory, 42–3

**morphology**, **50**

Morris water maze, 22, *23*, 24, 38, *39*
motor neurons in defensive reflex, 28–9

## N

N400 deviation, 75, 76
nausea, 17
neurofibrillary tangles, 24, *25*
neuronal firing, in working memory, *43*
neurons,
    interconnections in learning, 27–9
    *see also* postsynaptic neurons;
    presynaptic neurons
neurotransmitter release,
    in classical conditioning, 13, 14, 32–3
    Hebbian synapse, 34–6
neutral neuron, 13–14
**neutral stimulus**, *6*, **7**, 8, 11
nitric oxide, 36
NMDA receptors, 34–6
    protein synthesis, 39–42
noises, *54*, 55, 66
non-fluent aphasia, 68–70
non-speech sound, 66
**nouns**, **51**–2
    in anomia, 71–3
    phrases, 63

## O

**object**, **51**–2
object recognition memory, 37

## P

P600 deviation, 76
parietal cortex, lesions, *20*
parietal lobe, 72, 76
patients,
    agnosia, 19–20
    H.M., 18–19
    S., 44
patterning, duality of, 53–4
Pavlov, Ivan, 5–6, 11
Pavlovian conditioning, *see* classical
conditioning
paw lifting, dogs, 15–16
perirhinal cortex, *21*, 37
PET scanning, *73*
phobias, 17–18

**phonemes**, **53**, 54, 55
    identification, 58–60
    syllables, 57
**phonology**, **50**, 54–60
phrases, 63
pitch of sound, 54, 56
postsynaptic depolarization, 32–3, 35
postsynaptic neurons,
    firing, 12–13, 14
    long-term potentiation, 30, *31*, 35–6
practice makes perfect, 4, 13
prefrontal cortex, 42
preparedness, 17–18
prepositions, 51
presynaptic neurons,
    action potential, 12–13, 14
    long-term potentiation, 32–3, 35–6
primary auditory cortex, *65*, 66
probe test, 22, *39*
**procedural memory**, **4**–5
    patient H.M., 19
    rat conditioning, 9
protein synthesis, NMDA receptors, 39–42
punishments, in instrumental conditioning,
8, 11

## Q

quadrant test, 22, *39*

## R

radiotherapy, 17
rats,
    Garcia effect, 17
    instrumental conditioning, 8–10, 15, 16
    spatial learning, 22–4, 38, *39*
reflex response,
    blinking, 6–7, 8, 14
    salivation, 5–6
    in the sea slug, 27, *28*
reinforcement of behaviour, 8
resting membrane potentials, 34
retrograde amnesia, 3, 40
retrograde messengers, 36
rewards, in instrumental conditioning, 8–
10, 16
right hemisphere of the brain, 67

## S

salivation,
    classical conditioning, 32
    reflex response, 5–6
    role of Hebbian synapses, *14*
scrambled speech, 66
scrub jay (*Aphelocoma californica*),
brain, 21–2
sea slug (*Aplysia*), neurobiology of
learning, 27–9
**semantic memory**, **4**, *20*
**semantics**, **51**
    anomalies, 75, 76
    in fluent aphasia, 70–1
    problems with, 60–2
sensitization, 28–9
sensory neurons, in defensive reflex,
28–9
sentences,
    comprehension, 49
    ERP traces, 75
    in fluent aphasia, 70–1
    in non-fluent aphasia, 69–70
    spectrogram, *59*
    structure of, 62–3
    syntax, 50–1, 53–4, 60–1, 73
    three-stage processing, 76–7
sheep, electric shock, 11
short-term memory, 2–4
Skinner box, 8, *9*
snake, vervet monkey call, 49, 52, *55*, 60
sounds, 54–6
    mapping of, *65*, *66*
    *see also* speech
spatial learning,
    in mammals and birds, 21–4
    role of NMDA, 38, *39*
**specific language impairment**, **78**
spectrograms, *54*, *55*, *57*, *59*
speech, 49
    non-fluent aphasia, 68–9
    processing in the brain, 67–8
    *see also* sounds
speech perception, 64–7
spellings, 56
'split-brain' patients, 67
stimulus–response link, 9–10
Stromswold, Karin, 73

**subject**, **51**–2

Swedish mutation, in Alzheimer's disease, 25–6, 33, *34*

syllables, 57

synaptic connections in learning, 12–13, 27–9

synaptic depression, 37–8

synaptic efficiency, 13, 35

synaptic plasticity, 33, *34*

synaptic tagging, 40

**syntax**, **50**–1, 53–4, 60–1

    anomolies, 75–6

    problems with, 62–3, 69–70

    processing of, 73

**T**

tau protein, 24, *25*, 26

temporal categories of memory, *3*

temporal cortex, *37*

temporal lobe, 67, *68*, 72

temporal sulcus, *66*

thalamus, *40*, *65*

timbre, 55

**tonotopic** organization, **65**–6

transitive verbs, 51–2

trisynaptic circuit, *30*

**U**

unconditional neuron, *14*

**unconditional response**, *6*, **7**, 8

**unconditional stimulus**, *6*, **7**, 8, 11

**ungrammatical**, **50**–1

**V**

vampire bat, 17

verbal nouns, 51

**verbs**, **51**–2

    in aphasia, 73

vervet monkey (*Ceropithecus aethiops*), alarm call, 49, 52, *55*, 60

visuospatial working memory, 42

voice, *see* sounds; speech

**vowels**, **55**–6

    co-articulation, *59*

    identification, 58

**W**

water maze, 22, *23*, 24, 38, *39*

Wernicke's aphasia, 68, 70–3

Wernicke's area, 67–8

words, 51–2

    binding problem, 79

    duality of patterning, 53–4

    meanings of, 60–3

    memory recall, 1–2

**working memory**, **3**–4

    synaptic connections, 42–5